AWAY
—from—
HOME

Compiled by
Wendy Body & Pat Edwards

Acknowledgements

We are grateful to the following for permission to reproduce copyright material; Jonathan Cape Ltd for 'The Marvellous Ears' from *The BFG* by Roald Dahl, illustrated by Quentin Blake; William Collins Sons & Co Ltd for an extract from *The Homecoming* by Cynthia Voigt; the author's agents for an extract from *Up The Pier* by Helen Cresswell; Penguin Books Australia Ltd for an extract from *Elmer Runs Wild* by Patrick Cook.

We are grateful to the following for permission to reproduce photographs: AA Picture Library, page 79 *below left* and *below right*; Wendy Body, page 34 *above*; J Allan Cash, pages 79 *above left* and *centre right*; Crosfield Electronics Ltd, page 39 *above*; Dainippon Screen (UK), page 39 *below*; Alice Englander, page 36; Guernsey Maritime Trust, page 95; Michael Holford, pages 16, 17, 18, 19; Images Colour Library, page 79 *above right*; Northern Ireland Tourist Board, page 79 *centre left*; Dr Margaret Rule, C.B.E., F.S.A., pages 91, 92, 93, 94; States of Guernsey (Guernsey Museum and Art Gallery), drawing by Robert Reed, *background* for pages 90/91, 92/93, 94/95.

Illustrators, other than those acknowledged with each story, include Sisca pp. 1-3; Oxford Illustrators pp. 33-40; Helen Herbert pp. 64-7; Peter Schmidli pp. 48-9; Geoff Hocking pp. 80-9; Robert Reed pp. 90-5; Andrew Laws pp. 96-110.

Contents

Fife Council Education Department

King's Road Primary School

King's Crescent, Rosyth KY11 2RS

The Marvellous Ears

Back in the cave, the Big Friendly Giant sat Sophie down once again on the enormous table. "Is you quite snuggly there in your nightie?" he asked. "You isn't fridgy cold?"

"I'm fine," Sophie said.

"I cannot help thinking," said the BFG, "about your poor mother and father. By now they must be jipping and skumping all over the house shouting 'Hello hello where is Sophie gone?'"

"I don't have a mother and father," Sophie said. "They both died when I was a baby."

"Oh, you poor little scrumplet!" cried the BFG. "Is you not missing them very badly?"

"Not really," Sophie said, "because I never knew them."

"You is making me sad," the BFG said, rubbing his eyes.

"Don't be sad," Sophie said. "No one is going to be worrying too much about me. That place you took me from was the village orphanage. We are all orphans in there."

"You is a norphan?"

"Yes."

"How many is there in there?"

"Ten of us," Sophie said. "All little girls."

"Was you happy there?" the BFG asked.

"I hated it," Sophie said. "The woman who ran it was called Mrs Clonkers and if she caught you breaking any of the rules, like getting out of bed at night or not folding up your clothes, you got punished."

"How is you getting punished?"

"She locked us in the dark cellar for a day and a night without anything to eat or drink."

"The rotten old rotrasper!" cried the BFG.

"It was horrid," Sophie said. "We used to dread it. There were rats down there. We could hear them creeping about."

"The filthy old fizzwiggler!" shouted the BFG. "That is the horridest thing I is hearing for years! You is making me sadder than ever!" All at once, a huge tear that would have filled a bucket rolled down one of the BFG's cheeks and fell with a splash on the floor. It made quite a puddle.

Sophie watched with astonishment. What a strange and moody creature this is, she thought. One moment he is telling me my head is full of squashed flies and the next moment his heart is melting for me because Mrs Clonkers locks us in the cellar.

"The thing that worries *me*," Sophie said, "is having to stay in this dreadful place for the rest of my life. The orphanage was pretty awful, but I wouldn't have been there for ever, would I?"

"All is my fault," the BFG said. "I is the one who kidsnatched you." Yet another enormous tear welled from his eye and splashed on to the floor.

"Now I come to think of it, I won't actually be here all that long," Sophie said.

"I is afraid you will," the BFG said.

"No, I won't," Sophie said. "Those brutes out there are bound to catch me sooner or later and have me for tea."

"I is *never* letting that happen," the BFG said.

For a few moments the cave was silent. Then Sophie said, "May I ask you a question?"

The BFG wiped the tears from his eyes with the back of his hand and gave Sophie a long thoughtful stare. "Shoot away," he said.

"Would you please tell me what you were doing in our village last night? Why were you poking that long trumpet thing into the Goochey children's bedroom and then blowing through it?"

"Ah-ha!" cried the BFG, sitting up suddenly in his chair. "Now we is getting nosier than a parker!"

"And the suitcase you were carrying," Sophie said. "What on earth was *that* all about?"

The BFG stared suspiciously at the small girl sitting cross-legged on the table.

"You is asking me to tell you whoppsy big secrets," he said. "Secrets that nobody is ever hearing before."

"I won't tell a soul," Sophie said. "I swear it. How could I anyway? I am stuck here for the rest of my life."

"You could be telling the other giants."

"No, I couldn't," Sophie said. "You told me they would eat me up the moment they saw me."

"And so they would," said the BFG. "You is a human bean and human beans is like strawbunkles and cream to those giants."

"If they are going to eat me the moment they see me, then I wouldn't have time to tell them anything, would I?" Sophie said.

"You wouldn't," said the BFG.

"Then why did you say I might?"

"Because I is brimful of buzzburgers," the BFG said. "If you listen to everything I am saying you will be getting earache."

"Please tell me what you were doing in our village," Sophie said. "I promise you can trust me."

"Would you teach me how to make an elefunt?" the BFG asked.

"What *do* you mean?" Sophie said.

"I would dearly love to have an elefunt to ride on," the BFG said dreamily. "I would so much love to have a jumbly big elefunt and go riding through green forests picking peachy fruits off the trees all day long. This is a sizzling-hot muckfrumping country we is living in. Nothing grows in it except snozzcumbers. I would love to go somewhere else and pick peachy fruits in the early morning from the back of an elefunt."

Sophie was quite moved by this curious statement.

"Perhaps one day we will get you an elephant," she said. "And peachy fruits as well. Now tell me what you were doing in our village."

"If you is really wanting to know what I am doing in your village," the BFG said, "I is blowing a dream into the bedroom of those children."

"*Blowing a dream?*" Sophie said. "What *do* you mean?"

"I is a dream-blowing giant," the BFG said. "When all the other giants is galloping off every what way and which to swollop human beans, I is scuddling away to other places to blow dreams into the bedrooms of sleeping children. Nice dreams. Lovely golden dreams. Dreams that is giving the dreamers a happy time."

"Now hang on a minute," Sophie said. "Where do you get these dreams?"

"I collect them," the BFG said, waving an arm towards all the rows and rows of bottles on the shelves. "I has billions of them."

"You can't *collect* a dream," Sophie said. "A dream isn't something you can catch hold of."

"You is never going to understand about it," the BFG said. "That is why I is not wishing to tell you."

"Oh, please tell me!" Sophie said. "I *will* understand! Go on! Tell me how you collect dreams! Tell me everything!"

The BFG settled himself comfortably in his chair and crossed his legs. "Dreams," he said, "is very mysterious things. They is floating around in the air like little wispy-misty bubbles. And all the time they is searching for sleeping people."

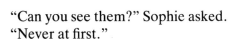

"Can you see them?" Sophie asked.

"Never at first."

"Then how do you catch them if you can't see them?" Sophie asked.

"Ah-ha," said the BFG. "Now we is getting on to the dark and dusky secrets."

"I won't tell a soul."

"I is trusting you," the BFG said. He closed his eyes and sat quite still for a moment, while Sophie waited.

"A dream," he said, "as it goes whiffling through the night air, is making a tiny little buzzing-humming noise. But this little buzzy-hum is so silvery soft, it is impossible for a human bean to be hearing it."

"Can *you* hear it?" Sophie asked.

The BFG pointed up at his enormous truck-wheel ears which he now began to move in and out. He performed this exercise proudly, with a little proud smile on his face. "Is you seeing these?" he asked.

"How could I miss them?" Sophie said.

"They maybe is looking a bit propsposterous to you," the BFG said, "but you must believe me when I say they is very extra-usual ears indeed. They is not to be coughed at."

"I'm quite sure they're not," Sophie said.

"They is allowing me to hear absolutely every single twiddly little thing."

"You mean you can hear things I can't hear?" Sophie said.

"You is *deaf as a dumpling* compared with me!" cried the BFG. "You is hearing only thumping loud noises with those little earwigs of yours. But I am hearing *all the secret whisperings of the world!*"

"Such as what?" Sophie asked.

"In your country," he said, "I is hearing the footsteps of a ladybird as she goes walking across a leaf."

"*Honestly?*" Sophie said, beginning to be impressed.

"What's more, I is hearing those footsteps *very loud*," the BFG said. "When a ladybird is walking across a leaf, I is hearing her feet going *clumpety-clumpety-clump* like giants' footsteps."

"Good gracious me!" Sophie said. "What else can you hear?"

"I is hearing the little ants chittering to each other as they scuddle around in the soil."

"You mean you can hear ants talking?"

"Every single word," the BFG said. "Although I is not exactly understanding their langwitch."

"Go on," Sophie said.

"Sometimes, on a very clear night," the BFG said, "and if I is swiggling my ears in the right direction," — and here he swivelled his great ears upwards so they were facing the ceiling — "if I is swiggling them like this and the night is very clear, I is sometimes hearing faraway music coming from the stars in the sky."

A queer little shiver passed through Sophie's body. She sat very quiet, waiting for more.

"My ears is what told me you was watching me out of your window last night," the BFG said.

"But I didn't make a sound," Sophie said.

"I was hearing your heart beating across the road," the BFG said. "Loud as a drum."

"Go on," Sophie said. "Please."

"I can hear plants and trees."

"Do *they* talk?" Sophie asked.

"They is not exactly talking," the BFG said. "But they is making noises. For instance, if I come along and I is picking a lovely flower, if I is twisting the stem of the flower till it breaks, then the plant is screaming. I can hear it screaming and screaming very clear."

"You don't mean it!" Sophie cried. "How awful!"

"It is screaming just like you would be screaming if someone was twisting *your* arm right off."

"Is that really true?" Sophie asked.

"You think I is swizzfiggling you?"

"It *is* rather hard to believe."

"Then I is stopping right here," said the BFG sharply. "I is not wishing to be called a fibster."

"Oh no! I'm not calling you anything!" Sophie cried. "I believe you! I do really! Please go on!"

The BFG gave her a long hard stare. Sophie looked right back at him, her face open to his. "I believe you," she said softly.

She had offended him, she could see that.

"I wouldn't ever be fibbling to you," he said.

"I know you wouldn't," Sophie said. "But you must understand that it isn't easy to believe such amazing things straightaway."

"I understand that," the BFG said.

"So do please forgive me and go on," she said.

He waited a while longer, and then he said, "It is the same with trees as it is with flowers. If I is chopping an axe into the trunk of a big tree, I is hearing a terrible sound coming from inside the heart of the tree."

"What sort of sound?" Sophie asked.

"A soft moaning sound," the BFG said. "It is like the sound an old man is making when he is dying slowly."

He paused. The cave was very silent.

"Trees is living and growing just like you and me," he said. "They is alive. So is plants."

He was sitting very straight in his chair now, his hands clasped tightly together in front of him. His face was bright, his eyes round and bright as two stars.

"Such wonderful and terrible sounds I is hearing!" he said. "Some of them you would never wish to be hearing yourself! But some is like glorious music!"

He seemed almost to be transfigured by the excitement of his thoughts. His face was beautiful in its blaze of emotions.

"Tell me some more about them," Sophie said quietly.

"You just ought to be hearing the little micies talking!" he said. "Little micies is always talking to each other and I is hearing them as loud as my own voice."

"What do they say?" Sophie asked.

"Only the micies know that," he said. "Spiders is also talking a great deal. You might not be thinking it but spiders is the most tremendous natterboxes. And when they is spinning their webs, they is singing all the time. They is singing sweeter than a nightingull."

"Who else do you hear?" Sophie asked.

"One of the biggest chatbags is the cattlepiddlers," the BFG said.

"What do they say?"

"They is argying all the time about who is going to be the prettiest butterfly. That is all they is ever talking about."

"Is there a dream floating around in here now?" Sophie asked.

The BFG moved his great ears this way and that, listening intently. He shook his head. "There is no dream in here," he said, "except in the bottles. I has a special place to go for catching dreams. They is not often coming to Giant Country."

"How do you catch them?"

"The same way you is catching butteryflies," the BFG answered. "With a net." He stood up and crossed over to a corner of the cave where a pole was leaning against the wall. The pole was about thirty feet long and there was a net on the end of it. "Here is the dream-catcher," he said, grasping the pole in one hand. "Every morning I is going out and snitching new dreams to put in my bottles."

Suddenly, he seemed to lose interest in the conversation. "I is getting hungry," he said. "It is time for eats."

Written by Roald Dahl
Illustrated by Quentin Blake

A FESTIVAL ABROAD

Photographs of the Venice Carnival

Elmer's country life

Elmer the rat lived in Mother Murphy's Fishburgers Take Away. Life was good. Then Mother Murphy's started to sell nothing but squid — no more golden fatty fish fingerettes or half finished buckets of greasy french fries. One night, Mother Murphy's caught fire and burned down. Elmer decided to take to the bush and soon finds himself a long way from home. So far, on his 'bush adventure' he's met an angry snake and a helpful koala. But stranger encounters lie ahead . . .

C antering over the hard and dusty paddock beyond the treeline, Elmer began to sweat. His tongue felt too big for his thirsty mouth and his stomach felt too small for comfort.

Elmer decided to find some shade and to lie down and get his wind and grumble to himself for a moment or two.

He swerved towards one of the dirty white bushes that littered the place and flung himself beneath it. Funny sort of bush. Soft and greasy, like a fisherman's hat. Then a voice spoke to Elmer from out of the bush.

"Baaaaaaaaa," it said.

For a second or two, as usual, Elmer panicked. First there were branches that turned snakey, and now this. Would a bush that bleated at him chase him up a tree as well?

"Baaa, mind your head. I nearly trod on it."

Elmer relaxed. The bush had his interests at heart.

"Sorry. I thought you were part of the plant life. I only ducked under here for shade."

"Plant life? You've been out in the sun too long. I'm just a sheep. A poor silly sheep. I'd rather be a bush, mind you. You wouldn't find a bush standing around all day, every day, waiting for the chopper. Would you? Maybe you would? Would they?"

The sheep appeared to have confused itself.

Elmer turned on the charm.

"What's your name?"

"Name? Name? Aaaahhh . . . don't have it on me at present. Ethel? Andrew? Something like that, I think?"

Elmer decided to try some easier questions.

"Anything to drink around here?"

"Drink? No, hasn't been for months. Sometimes you can smell a river or a creek or something when the wind's right. But it's way over there on the other side of the house."

The sheep turned to face the house. All over the paddock the other sheep turned and faced the house, too.

"Sometimes the people pour a bit of water in a tin thingie for us. Over there. I don't know whether they'd turn it on for a rat, though."

"What about rain?"

"Luxury. I've never seen any. I've served this paddock lamb and sheep for six whole months, and I've never seen any. The older sheep remember it. Rain. I dream of rain. Even a drizzle."

"Anything to eat, then?"

"You're standing on it. Bit dry for my taste, but there you are. It helps to pass the time."

"Grass?"

"Yes, it's grass. What else would you eat?"

"Anything except grass and leaves and Bran Surprises."

"Not grass, then?"

The sheep took a step backwards in amazement. Every other sheep for a mile around took a step back.

"No, no, no. Real food. People food. Pink cakes and green pasties and orange spare ribs and old chutney and lamb sandwi . . ."

Elmer stopped himself. The sheep was looking at him strangely. A thought was wrestling with itself inside its tiny mind.

"Lamb sandwi . . ."

Elmer started to move away.

"Er . . . yes."

"What's a lamb sandwi . . .?"

"Well, you know, bread and . . . er . . . sort of meat."

"Meat? I'm meat? Aren't I? I am!"

The sheep was really thinking now. Elmer could practically hear the cogs in its brain rotate.

"So," said the sheep, "that's what they do with it. I stand around in the sun for months and months, putting up with dry grass and nothing to drink and bad haircuts, and after I go to the chopper I get fed to rats!"

Elmer was almost as shocked as the sheep was. He'd put away a fair bit of meat in his time, but he'd never had a conversation with it.

"Not just rats. There's . . . er . . . seagulls, for instance."

"Seagulls," the sheep didn't bother to ask what seagulls were. The sheep was extremely cross. "Rameses!"

A very large sheep nearby, with hard, curly yellow horns, turned to them impatiently. All the other sheep turned to them as well.

"What is it now?"

"This rat's trying to eat me."

The sheep with the horns lowered its head. Teeth showed. Nostrils flared. Rameses accelerated. Elmer took off. Rameses pounded across the turf. Elmer hardly touched it. All the other sheep did what other sheep do. They followed the sheep in front. Away across the paddock, his frenzied paws kicking up little puffs of dust, ran Elmer, followed by a sheep stampede.

He reached the fence.

"Hurray," thought Elmer as he ducked under the wire, "Safety!"

"Crunch," went the fencepost as the whole fence was swept away by a ton of fast moving sheep.

"Kerboom!" went a shotgun.

A shotgun! Elmer knew all about shotguns. He'd met one once when he interrupted a card game in a Chinese restaurant. It had taken him all night to pick the pellets out. He'd never gone hunting for crispy noodles since. Elmer turned sharp left.

"Kerboom!"

The kerboom frightened the sheep as well. The sheep in front tried to stop. The sheep behind fell over them. They all rolled about and kicked and bleated in terror for a moment or so, then staggered to their dozens of feet and stampeded off in the reverse direction.

Elmer ducked under a tractor.

Peering out he saw a man and a woman in loud check shirts and big dusty hats. The trousers were not visible, but Elmer guessed dusty blue. The woman was still aiming a smoking shotgun at the sky.

"What got into those fool sheep?"

"Dunno. That fence has had it."

"So have we if we're not careful," the man sniffed the hot breeze, "you can smell it, can't you?"

"I smelled it yesterday."

"Well, I felt it in me bones last Thursday."

"Well, I had a dream about it the week before Christmas last."

They wandered off, squabbling.

Elmer was curious. What were they worried about? All around the homestead the trees were peaceful and dusty green. Beyond them the hills rolled gracefully, blue and serene. The usual birds warbled. Apart from the terrible shortage of food, the country seemed a calm and open place. There were none of the disgusting cars, none of the awful people-boxes, none of the endless noise. These people didn't know when they were well off. And what did they sniff the breeze for? Elmer sniffed, too.

His heart swelled with joy. Pie! Shepherd's pie!

Elmer darted from tractor to haybale to water trough, following his nose in the general direction of pie. At the trough he hung over the edge by his heels for a moment and sucked up some dirty brown water. He was so thirsty that it tasted better than cola, better than a warm, sticky orange drink with cigarette butts in it, much better than no water at all.

Wiping his whiskers he scuttled across the yard and hopped up onto the verandah of the house. He sneaked along the verandah from one hiding place to another. The house was a low, rambling sort of building. The verandah ran all the way around it and was littered and cluttered and heaped with shovels and bags of fertiliser and boots and parts of old cars. The farmers stood in the driveway. They stared at the hills. Beyond the hills rose a thin plume of smoke.

"There's some lucky devil over there cooking lunch," thought Elmer.

The farmers tipped back their hats together, shook their heads in unison, adjusted their respective blue trousers and spat into the dust.

"Better do something about that fence."

"Better. Dunno why we bother."

"Best to keep busy."

They sloped off towards the broken fence.

Yippee! Alone at last, Elmer sauntered through a hole in a fly screen door, bold as brass, and followed his trusty nose to the kitchen.

Bingo! Up on the windowsill was a pie. It was crusty with potato. It was steaming. Right next to it was a tray of fat, fresh pumpkin scones. They were steaming too. A picture of heaven for a rat.

Elmer stuck his elbow in the pie to test the temperature. Too hot. He reached for a scone instead. Another paw beat him to it. Elmer gasped. Another rat gasped right back. Two rats stared at each other, astonished. Elmer heard a low, bloodthirsty growl. They breed a tough rat out here, he thought.

Snap! The very tiny tip of Elmer's tail disappeared between the teeth of a large, red-eyed cattle dog.

"Eeearrrggghhh! Ouch! Raargh!"

Over the pie and out the window Elmer sprang. He bounced off the verandah and hared across a dead vegetable patch for the safety of the scrub.

He banged into rocks and he floundered into creepers and he tangled with bushes and he was very sore in the tail department. He hurled his battered person behind a log. He heard the dog snarfling and grumpling about for a while and then he heard the dog going away.

"Ouch," said Elmer about his tail. There was a little bit missing and a little bit of blood. He'd had worse, but that didn't stop it hurting and he was still hungry.

"So much for the country," he snorted, "if I had wanted mad dogs and not enough to eat, I could have stayed at home".

Then he remembered that he didn't have one. He was alone in a strange place. He sniffled. He felt hounded and abused and sorry for himself. The grass rustled. A cough. What next? What would they do to him now? The strange rat that he had seen on the window sill strolled out of the grass. The strange rat was holding a pumpkin scone.

The strange rat smiled.

"G'day."

"G'day," said Elmer, right back. He was relieved. The new rat didn't seem to be dangerous and the pumpkin scone seemed to be downright friendly. Even so, Elmer did not feel altogether comfortable.

"You're sitting in a clump of bindis," said the new rat.

"Am I?" said Elmer, "I am. Ouch!"

He hopped up, picking at the nasty little burrs and flinching at the twinges. Some of the bindis were in that little spot in the middle of the back that you can't quite reach.

"Roll on to your front," said the new rat, "I'll get 'em out".

Elmer was alarmed by this kindness. The last rat who had done him a favour had been one of those breakfast-hating rats and he had upended Elmer in a tin of cold water.

"Why . . . er, that is, thanks but why?"

"You drew the dog away. I know you didn't mean to, but I owe you a favour anyway."

Elmer rolled over. A few twinges later he was bindi free. He enjoyed the feeling.

"I'm Elmer," he announced formally.

"I'm Alma," said the helpful rat, "like Elmer with two 'a's. Have some scone."

Elmer did. This was unexpected. His sisters were never this generous. Neither were his brothers. Or his parents. Or his friends, except when there was too much to eat. Most rats are like that.

"I'm a city rat," he went on, "what about yourself? Country?"

"Not as such. I used to live in a truck with some people."

"With people?" Elmer didn't believe it.

"With musicians. They used to travel about and make music. Very loud."

"They didn't stomp on you?"

"They used to feed me by hand," Alma was proud of it, "They used to sleep on the floor of the truck with their eyes open. Weird. They said I was good luck."

"Were you?"

"Dunno. I wasn't good luck on the day the truck blew up. They all just walked away."

"And now you're sort of a bush rat?"

"Not really. You haven't met any bush rats. Otherwise you'd know why I'm pleased to see another city rat. I hung around the house for food until the dog noticed me."

"I don't like that dog," Elmer fingered his tail carefully, "I think it's disturbed".

"It is, and it's right behind you."

Elmer swivelled. The dog was right behind him. The rats jumped the log. Then there was a high pitched whistle.

"Peeewhiiitt!"

The dog froze, digested the whistle, performed a U-turn and barked back to the house. Standing on the log, Elmer could hear the farmer arguing in the ute.

"That darned dog,"

"Watch it. That's my dog."

"It'll be a barbequed dog tomorrow," said the farmer. He jerked a thumb towards the hills where the plume of smoke was bigger and blacker. "It's coming. I can feel it in my sinuses."

"I can feel it in my joints."

"I can feel it in the wind up my nostrils."

Feel what? Elmer wondered. The dog ended the squabble by bounding out of the bush, tongue around its ankles, yarping happily. The woman whistled the dog into the ute. There was the sound of a dog being belted around the ear. The ute was crunched into gear and screeched off in a cloud of dust and rubber.

"It's all go, here," said Elmer, "and they've gone. Let's explore that pie."

"Too risky. They've only gone to chop up a sheep or something. They'll be back. We might try later."

"Oh," Elmer was disappointed. So near a pie and yet so far.

"Are you hungry? Let's get some bush food."

Was Elmer hungry! Do birds fly? Do fish swim? Do fishermen smell?

Alma led the way. She was glad of the company and eager to show off her bush skills.

"What are bush rats like?" asked Elmer, as he puffed his way up a steep fall of rocks and stopped at a small ravine.

"Mad, bad and dangerous to get close to," answered Alma, who swung nimbly over the ravine on a low lying branch and landed on the other side on one graceful foot. "They're twice the size of us, they've forgotten how to talk, and they eat each other when times are tough. They're almost as bad as people."

"Disgusting," said Elmer as he missed the branch, the rock and his footing, and fell gracefully onto his head a few feet below. Alma forked him out with a stick.

"It is hard at first, the bush," she said.

"How long is 'at first'," Elmer wondered, "when does it stop hurting?"

He was good at dodging cars and trucks and people and other moving objects, but he wasn't good with rocks and roots and branches which kept still and then reached up to grab him.

"Sssshhh!" Alma grabbed Elmer and forced him into the ground. She put a paw to her lips and pointed. Elmer spat out a little soil and gaped.

Just ahead, in a clearing at the base of a tree, was a small blood-stained heap of dead rabbits. Who piles up dead rabbits? A dog? A dog!

A rustle in the grass, the soft pad of paws and a small red dog with a swishy tail trotted into view and deposited another dead rabbit.

"Dog," squeaked Elmer.

"Fox," hissed Alma.

"And a fox with a big feed in mind."

She continued to surprise Elmer; without much of a sound she slithered through the grass on her belly, popped up right behind the fox and dinged a pebble off the back of his neck.

The fox yiked, leaped and disappeared.

Elmer was horrified.

"That fox won't like us!"

"Shut up. Come on," Alma darted across the clearing. Elmer followed fearfully. Alma dragged the littlest dead rabbit from the pile.

"Grab the front."

"Why?"

"DO IT!"

Two rats, one urgent and one confused, lugged a dead rabbit back into the scrub.

"On, on, on!"

Back down the hill they rolled and scrambled, doubled back up the hill to the left, down, up, down, right, left, right, and fetched up against a sheer rock wall.

"That'll throw the fox off our tails," said Alma, pleased with herself. She dropped her end of the rabbit and heaved away at a fallen bush. Behind it was a little cave.

"In, in, in!"

Elmer pushed the rabbit in, Alma pushed Elmer in and followed him. She dragged the bush behind her, sealing off the cave. Inside, a little light trickled through the branches, but Elmer found it too dark, too small and too full of rabbit.

"What about the fox?"

"Arrr. Gutless. Foxes are gun-shy. That one probably thought it had been shot."

"Great, and what about the — er — rabbit?"

"Tuck in."

"*Eat* it? Dead? Raw?"

"Of course, eat it. What did you think we were going to do with it, stupid? Give it a decent funeral?"

Elmer boggled at the thought. He already felt like a body snatcher. He didn't want to feel like some sort of cannibal.

"I can't."

Alma had started without him, tearing into the rabbit's near hind leg with sharp little teeth. There was blood on her snout.

"Why not? You're not a poor silly sheep or a koala in disguise are you? Rats eat meat. This is meat."

"Yes. No. Not like this."

Alma was very annoyed. She'd gone to a lot of trouble to prepare this meal and it wasn't going to go to waste.

"What about that pie? What was in that?"

"Not recently alive rabbits."

"No. Recently alive sheep, that's what. Baaaa! Your friends — walking and talking today, eaten tomorrow."

Elmer thought about this.

"I think it's the fur. I've got fur myself. I think I prefer them in pastry."

Alma controlled her temper. She understood. It had been like that for her at first. She handed a rabbit's leg to Elmer.

"Rabbit's foot. Good Luck. It's that or nothing."

By now Elmer was starving. He took a little nibble. It was raw, but it was food. He wasn't sure about the taste of blood at first, but he closed his eyes and gnawed and tugged and chewed and swallowed.

"It's only hard at first," Alma patted his paw, "It was the same for me. If you're going to live in the bush, you've got to be a bit wild."

"Wild?" Elmer didn't think he had been wild before. He certainly felt cheerful after some food, and raw red rabbit juice had a kind of zing in it. Wild? He tried to growl. He burped instead and giggled. He tried again and surprised himself with a deep silky growl. Except that it wasn't him.

A red paw swept aside the branches. A red muzzle poked into the cave.

"Absolutely typical! Rats! Thieving little vermin!"

Elmer wiped a dribble of rabbit juice from his whiskers. He didn't feel scared. He felt like a fight.

"Rack off, bushy bottom," he heard himself snarl at the fox, "or I'll take a piece out of you".

"You," said the fox, backing away slightly, "you're not even a bush rat. You're a mouse!"

This is a pretty big insult to a rat.

"Try me!" Elmer bared his not very big fangs.

"Certainly not. Who knows where city rats have been. If I ate you, I could catch something."

Alma stepped in. It was just as well. The effect of raw meat was wearing off. Elmer began to notice signs of indigestion and to wonder whether he'd gone too far.

"You finish it off," Alma told the fox. "We're full."

"Barp," burped Elmer.

"I will," said the fox. With half a dozen quick, crunching chomps the rabbit disappeared, bones, fur, cottontail and all. Elmer's insides turned over. He wasn't a fussy eater by any means, but this fox was a real animal.

"In any case," said the fox, "I suppose a runt like you couldn't catch and kill a mosquito, much less a rabbit".

"Catch," said Elmer, "and kill? Certainly not. I'm not that cruel."

"Cruel? What's cruel? You ate the rabbit, didn't you? Besides, they like it really."

"How could they . . ."

The fox smiled, a smile of a pleasant memory.

"They love it. The thrill of the chase. The wind in their whiskers."

"I bet they don't. Think of how much it hurts."

"Ah yes," the fox sighed, "you always hurt the one you love to eat".

He reminded Elmer a lot of the mad, yellow-toothed dog. Elmer decided to change the subject.

"Nice hill you've got for it. For hunting."

The fox narrowed two bright and wicked eyes.

"Take a good look, city mouse, a quick look. Because if you're still here tomorrow, I might have to tell the bush rats where you are. Goodbye. Have a nice day."

A whisk of the red tail and the grey grasses swallowed up the fox.

"How did the fox know I was a city rat?"

"Perhaps it was your accent. We'd better go. He meant that about the bush rats. To a bush rat, you're a rabbit."

Alma said goodbye to her cave. Now they were both homeless. Down the hill plodded two discontented rats. The late afternoon sun had sunk behind the hills, although there was an hour or two of light left to travel. The dusty trees threw long shadows on the paddocks. The colours were deeper, green and grey and deep blue beyond. Elmer remembered the city. People would be escaping from the horrible people-boxes by now, piling into their car boxes and their bus boxes which would blurt and farfle smoke and fumes until the air was full of dirt and noise. It was a good time of the day for rat snacks, half-eaten waffle bars chucked away in parks, last minute chips before dinners and so on.

Elmer didn't really miss any of that. He liked the view and the air and the patterns of the leaves. He liked them for at least ten minutes. Then he remembered the pie.

Illustrated and written by Patrick Cook

○ Britain

○ Kuala Lumpur

○ Hong Kong

Printed a long way from home

How a book is made

> You probably enjoy reading but have you ever thought how long it takes to produce a book for you to read? There are many stages and lots of people who are involved.

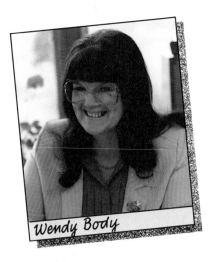

Wendy Body

Wendy Body, who has written for *Longman Reading World*, says this about her writing:

" I get ideas for stories in all kinds of ways. For example, *The Bracelet*, which is in Level 3, came about because I always wear a bracelet and when I'm thinking I often fiddle around with it. I found myself doing this one day and suddenly began wondering what it would be like to have a magic bracelet which would do various things if you touched different stones. That's how the story got started! Writing can be hard sometimes. I keep working at a story and changing things until I'm satisfied. Just like you, I go through the stages of composing or drafting a story, revising and then editing it — that's when I check my spelling, punctuation and so on. Finally I type it out and send the manuscript off to the publisher. **"**

David Jamieson

At the publishing house, the **publisher**, David Jamieson, reads the manuscript, and if he is happy with it, passes it on to the editors.

The **editors** check the manuscript to make sure that nothing is missing, that it all makes sense and is grammatically correct. They also write down details of what illustrations they think would look good.

The **designers** look carefully at the manuscript and write instructions on it for the typesetter. They tell the typesetter what typeface to use, how big it should be, how long to make the lines and where to leave spaces. There are many different typefaces, which have all been carefully designed. For *The Bracelet*, the designer decided to use a typeface call **Gill Sans**.

The **production controller** checks that all the instructions for the typesetter are clear, and sends the manuscript off to be set. *Longman Reading World* books are typeset in Kuala Lumpur and although the typesetters speak English, the instructions must be very clear and legible.

The **typesetter** types all the words and instructions into a computer which prints them out onto a long strip of photosensitive paper called a galley. He makes a copy or "proof" of this and sends it back for the editor and designer to check. The editor checks that all the words are spelt correctly and that nothing has been missed out. The designer makes sure that the typeface and spacing are correct. The proof is returned to the typesetter for the corrections to be done.

What was it the magpie bird had said? "This is for you but not just for you, so that you can do what you have to do." "This is very strange"! Kamala thought Kamala put the bracelet on her arm. She looked at it and then "It's lovely" she (said to herself)

Page 8   Type in 18/24 Gill Sans Medium

What was it the magpie had said?
"This is for you but not just for you,
so that you can do what you have to do."
It was very strange! Kamala put the bracelet on her
arm. She looked at it and then said to herself:
"It's lovely."

E
Gill Sans
Medium

E
Beton
Bold

E
Cloister Cursive
Handtooled

E
Hawthorn

𝕰
Old English
Text

What was it the magpie had said?
"This is for you but not just for you,
so that you can do what you have to do."
It was very strange! Kamala put the bracelet on her
arm. She looked at it and then said to herself,
"It's lovely."

Galley proof

35

Alice Englander

What was it the magpie had said?
"This is for you but not just for you,
so that you can do what you have to do."

It was very strange! Kamala put the bracelet on her
arm. She looked at it and then said to herself,
"It's lovely."

Make hair
into a plait

Photocopy of rough
artwork with galley
proof in position

Finished artwork

Meanwhile, the illustrations for the story are prepared.
The designer finds a suitable illustrator and arranges
for sketches called "roughs" to be drawn. The author,
editor and designer check the roughs to make sure that
they are happy with the style and also that the details
are correct.

Once the galley proofs and the roughs have arrived,
the designer prepares a "rough paste-up". Using paper
that is printed with a page-plan or "grid", the designer
sticks the roughs and galley proofs onto it so that she
can see if there are going to be any problems fitting
everything in, and whether it looks good or not. If the
roughs are alright, the illustrator is told to go ahead and
prepare the finished artwork.

The artwork is often prepared bigger than it will
actually appear in the finished book. This is because the
quality of the picture is usually better if it is reduced in
size when it is printed. The designer decides with the
illustrator how much bigger the pictures will be drawn.

When the typesetter has corrected the mistakes marked on the galley proof, he makes a correct print-out from the computer and sends this to the editor and designer to check again. The editor checks that all the mistakes have been corrected and the designer checks that the galley is clean and undamaged so that it will photograph well.

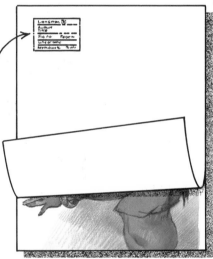

Photocopy of artwork reduced to correct size and positioned as a guide for the printer

Once both the corrected galleys and the artwork have arrived the designer prepares the book for the printer. The finished artwork is photocopied (reducing it to the correct size) and stuck carefully onto the grid paper. A photocopy of the text is stuck in position as well. The printer uses this as a guide for making up the pages. The designer labels each piece of artwork to show the page on which it is to appear and the size it is to be. She puts the artwork with the corrected galleys.

When everything is ready, it is checked by the editor, and also double-checked by the production controller, who makes sure that all the instructions are clear for the printer. He then sends the package off to the printer.

Artwork with protective paper overlay.

Artwork identification stamp

Longman

Author *Wendy Body*
Title *The Bracelet*

Fig no 5   Page no 8

Line or tone: *4 colour tone*

Reproduce to *67* % of original size

The pages of *The Bracelet* were arranged like this:

1	48	45	4	5	44
24	25	28	21	20	29
13	36	33	17	16	32
12	37	40	9	8	41

43	6	3	47	46	2
30	19	22	27	26	23
31	18	15	35	34	14
42	7	10	39	38	11

The printer follows the instructions and makes up the pages of the book. He works out how to arrange the pages so that they will fit onto the large sheets of printing paper. The pages are arranged so that when the sheet is folded up after printing, each page will appear in the right place.

The printer uses special photographic equipment to transfer the artwork and text onto film. For colour books, four different pieces of film must be made for each page, one for each of the following colours: cyan (blue), magenta (pink), yellow and black. A full colour book is made up of a combination of these four colours.

If you look at a colour picture in a book through quite a strong magnifying glass, you can see that it is made up of lots of tiny dots of the four colours. If the dots of one colour are close together, that colour will be darker. If they are smaller and further apart, the colour will be lighter.

From each sheet of film, a printing plate is made by pressing together the film and a thin metal photosensitive plate, and exposing them to strong light. The light shines through the transparent areas of the film but cannot shine through the dark areas.

The parts of the plate which are exposed to the light change so that the image on the film is transferred to the plate. The exposed areas will now hold ink which will print on the paper.

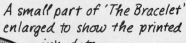

A small part of 'The Bracelet' enlarged to show the printed ink dots

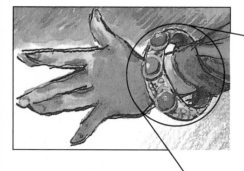

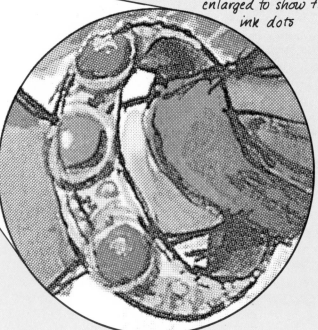

The printer prints a few "proof" copies of the book to send back to the editor, designer and production controller who give them one final check for mistakes and quality. The colours are proofed in the following sequence: cyan; cyan and magenta; cyan, magenta and yellow; cyan, magenta, yellow and black. These are called "progressive" proofs. Corrections can then be made to the plates if necessary, before the printer goes ahead and prints the number of books required. For *The Bracelet*, the "print-run" was fifteen thousand.

A Colour Scanner
This transfers the four colours from the artwork or photograph onto separate pieces of film.

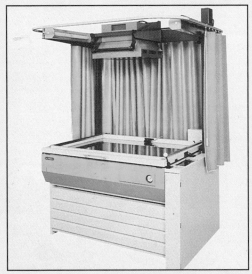

A Print-down frame
This is where the printing plates are made.

Plate-making

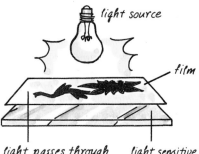

light source

film

light passes through clear parts of film to plate beneath

light sensitive metal plate

yellow

magenta

cyan

black

cyan and magenta

cyan, magenta and yellow

cyan, magenta, yellow and black

A set of progressive proofs from 'The Bracelet'

39

The four-colour printing process

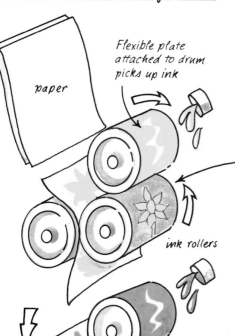

paper

Flexible plate
attached to drum
picks up ink

ink rollers

As each sheet of paper passes through the printing machine, the coloured inks from the four different plates are printed one on top of the other. After the sheets have been printed, they are folded by machine and the cover (printed separately) is put on. The book is stapled together through the spine and trimmed neatly around the three edges.

Image transferred
to this roller and
then to paper

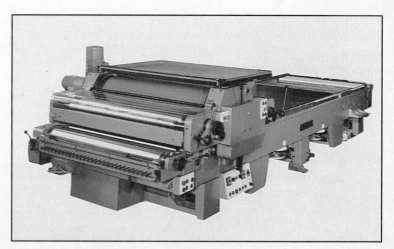

A Proofing Press

The Bracelet, like other *Longman Reading World* books, was printed in Hong Kong. It takes eight weeks for the books to be shipped back to the warehouse in Harlow, Essex. From there they are sent out to schools or bookshops. Your book travelled a very long way before it reached you!

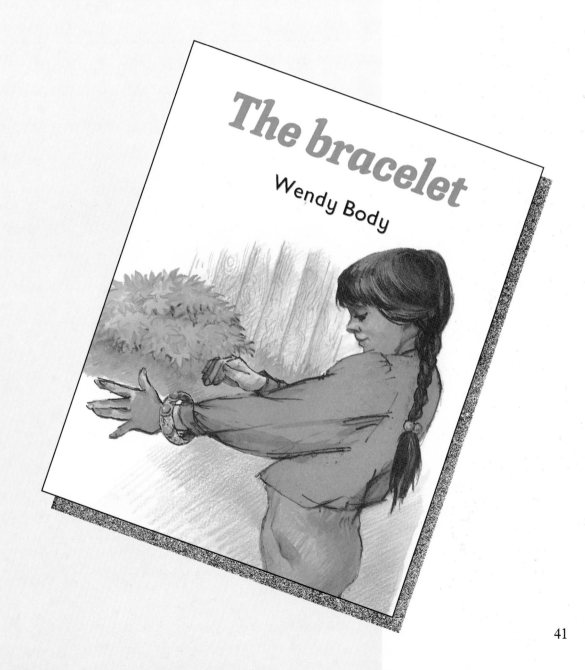

A Stormy Day

There are many instances of inherited writing
talent and Anna Sewell (1820–1878) is one of
them. Her mother was an early Victorian
versifier who wrote long moralizing poems in
a simple ballad form that sold enormously.
Anna injured both ankles when very young
and was a semi-invalid for most of her life.
Her odd but excellent idea of writing "the
autobiography of a horse" was inspired by
her wish to make people kinder to their
horses. In those days, of course, horses were
everywhere, for they were made to do the
work that motor cars and tractors do now.
"Black Beauty" was a great success in France,
Italy and Germany as well as in Britain, and
the Royal Society for the Prevention of
Cruelty to Animals praised it highly — an
unusual recommendation for a book. Here
Black Beauty recounts the tale of an exciting
night:

ONE day late in the autumn, my master had a long journey to go on business. I was put into the dog-cart, and John went with his master. I always liked to go in the dog-cart; it was so light, and the high wheels ran along so pleasantly. There had been a great deal of rain, and now the wind was very high and blew the dry leaves across the road in a shower. We went along merrily till we came to the toll-bar and the low wooden bridge. The river banks were rather high, and the bridge, instead of rising, went across just level, so that in the middle, if the river was full, the water would be nearly up to the wood-work and planks; but as there were good substantial rails on each side, people did not mind it.

The man at the gate said the river was rising fast, and he feared it would be a bad night. Many of the meadows were under water, and in one low part of the road the water was halfway up to my knees; the bottom was good, and master drove gently, so it was no matter.

When we got to the town, of course, I had a good feed, but as the master's business engaged him a long time, we did not start for home till rather late in the afternoon. The wind was then much higher, and I heard the master say to John he had never been out in such a storm; and so I thought, as we went along the skirts of a wood, where great branches were swaying about like twigs, and the rushing sound was terrible.

"I wish we were well out of this wood," said my master.

"Yes, sir," said John, "it would be rather awkward if one of these branches came down upon us." The words were scarcely out of his mouth, when there was a groan, and a crack and a splitting sound, and tearing, crashing down amongst the other trees, came an oak, torn up by the roots, and it fell right across the road just before us. I will never say I was not frightened, for I was. I stopped still, and I believe I trembled; of course I did not turn round or run away; I was not brought up to that. John jumped out and was in a moment at my head.

"That was a very near touch," said my master. "What's to be done now?"

"Well, sir, we can't drive over that tree nor yet round it; there will be nothing for it but to go back to the four crossways, and that will be a good six miles before we get round to the wooden bridge again; it will make us late, but the horse is fresh." So back we went, and round by the crossroads; but by the time we got to the bridge, it was very nearly dark and we could just see that the water was over the middle of it; but as that happened sometimes when the floods were out, master did not stop. We were going along at a good pace, but the moment my feet touched the first part of the bridge I felt sure there was something wrong. I dare not go forward and I made a dead stop.

"Go on, Beauty," said my master and he gave me a touch with the whip, but I dare not stir; he gave me a sharp cut, I jumped, but I dare not go forward.

"There's something wrong, sir," said John, and he sprang out of the dog-cart, and came to my head and looked all about. He tried to lead me forward.

"Come on, Beauty, what's the matter?" Of course I could not tell him, but I knew very well that the bridge was not safe.

Just then the man at the toll-gate on the other side ran out of the house, tossing a torch about like one mad.

"Hoy, hoy, hoy, halloo, stop!" he cried.

"What's the matter?" shouted my master.

"The bridge is broken in the middle and part of it is carried away; if you come on you'll be into the river."

"Thank God!" said my master.

"You Beauty!" said John, and took the bridle and gently turned me round to the right-hand road by the river-side. The sun had set some time, the wind seemed to have lulled off after that furious blast which tore up the tree. It grew darker and darker, stiller and stiller. I trotted quietly along, the wheels hardly making a sound on the soft road. For a good while neither master nor John spoke, and then master began in a serious voice. I could not understand much of what they said, but I found they thought, if I had gone on as the master wanted me, most likely the bridge would have given way under us, and horse, chaise, master, and man would have fallen into the river; and as the current was flowing very strongly, and there was no light and no help at hand, it was more than likely we should all have been drowned. Master said God had given men reason by which they could find out things for themselves, but He had given animals knowledge which did not depend on reason, and which was much more prompt and perfect in its way, and by which they had often saved the lives of men. John had many stories to tell of dogs and horses, and the wonderful things they had done; he thought people did not value their animals half enough, nor make friends of them as they ought to do. I am sure he makes friends of them if ever a man did.

At last we came to the Park gates, and found the gardener looking out for us. He said that mistress had been in a dreadful way ever since dark, fearing some accident had happened, and that she had sent James off on Justice, the roan cob, to make inquiry after us.

We saw a light at the hall door and at the upper windows, and as we came up, mistress ran out, saying, "Are you really safe, my dear? Oh! I have been so anxious, fancying all sorts of things. Have you had no accident?"

"No, my dear; but if your Black Beauty had not been wiser than we were, we should all have been carried down the river at the wooden bridge." I heard no more, as they went into the house, and John took me to the stable. Oh! what a good supper he gave me that night: a good bran mash and some crushed beans with my oats, and such a thick bed of straw, and I was glad of it, for I was tired.

Written by Anna Sewell
Illustrated by Sara Woodward

The long way home for Odysseus

Who was Odysseus?

Super hero of Greek mythology — that's who! Of all the heroes, he was the greatest. So what was he like, this chieftain who called himself King of Ithaca? Tall? Handsome as a Greek god? The John Wayne of the Mediterranean? Well actually, he was red headed, short legged and easily conned by a pretty woman. But he was a wily and careful fighter, best at planning of all those who commanded their soldiers at the battle of Troy and he was without doubt, the most indomitable voyager of all time.

His adventures, described in *The Odyssey* by the blind Greek poet Homer, have been told and retold for hundreds of years simply because they are such a rattling good story. In fact, this epic poem which spreads over twenty-four books, has often been called 'the first novel ever written and, perhaps the best'.

What was his voyage?

Simply from Troy back to Ithaca. The seige of Troy was finally over after ten weary years of fighting and everyone was heading home to waiting wives and families who'd presumably been getting on with life while the soldiers fought the enemy and bickered amongst themselves. And being human, they took all the credit for the victory on themselves, forgetting they'd often been helped out of a tight spot by the gods *Poseidon* and Athena. Miffed about not being given more credit, these two decided to teach the homeward-bound chiefs a lesson.

Poseidon (who is god of the sea) stirs up a fearful storm which scatters their ships and drowns many of the crew. Odysseus is hit worst of all, so hopelessly off track he has no idea where he is. And from then on, thanks to the interference of Athena and Poseidon, things continually go wrong.

During the next three years he and his men island-hop their way around the Aegean Sea, meeting an incredible bunch of characters as they go. There are the Lotus Eaters (who feed on fruit that makes them forget their former lives), the one-eyed Cyclop with a taste for human flesh, King *Aeolus* of the Country of the Winds (he's able to stuff the storm winds in a sack, but of course some clot lets them out), giant cannibals who eat everyone except those on Odysseus's ship and Circe, the charmer with the unfortunate habit of turning men into animals. Odysseus tames her, of course, and after dallying awhile (a whole year, would you believe?) is off again. Next port of call is Hades (to ask a prophet the way home), then it's on past the Island of Sirens (their song drives men mad with desire), dodging Scylla a sea monster and Charybdis a whirlpool, before calling in at the Island of the Sun.
There, while Odysseus is busy elsewhere, his men decide to have a barbecue with the sun's sacred oxen. Vengeance is swift. A thunderbolt shatters the ship and everyone drowns except — you've guessed it, good old Odysseus! He clings to the keel, rides out the storm and is finally cast up on an island belonging to the goddess Calypso. She takes one look at our short red-head and decides he's the answer to her maidenly prayers. Poor Odysseus is kept prisoner for the next seven years.

At last Athena feels it's time the aging hero was allowed to go and gets Zeus to arrange it. Free at last Odysseus heads for home but — wouldn't you know it — Poseidon, who's still holding a grudge sees to it that he's shipwrecked again. But this time he's in luck and falls in with a good, sensible king who has a daughter with the revolting name of Nausicaa. They take him back to Ithaca.

Meanwhile, back at the ranch (or rather, the palace)... but there's a whole new story in what's been happening to Penelope, Odysseus's wife during the past twenty years, not to mention his son Telemachus , who's been searching for his long lost dad.

If you want to know that and the exciting end to the saga (disguise, trickery, challenge, suspense, a contest with a climax dripping in gore)...then you'll have to read it for yourself!

Why should we remember Odysseus?

The story of the Odyssey crops up in all Western literature. Over the years, people have fallen into the habit of describing any long, wandering journey or undertaking as an odyssey. The character of Odysseus is fascinating as he's no paper hero — he could be teacherous and cruel as well as noble and brave. Most interesting of all, unlike most mythical Greek heroes he solved his problems by using his intellect instead of through magically-given physical strength. He was the first great modern hero.

KIDS HAVE NO LEGAL RIGHTS?

Thirteen year old Dicey Tillerman knew there was something wrong with her mother. The sudden decision to pack up and leave in the middle of the night to visit a relative they've never met had made Dicey feel uneasy. Even though they were all used to being a one-parent family, you didn't have to be very old to realise what a strain it was on that parent. Yet Dicey had never expected her mother to abandon them all in a shopping mall car park in a strange city. Reluctantly, she realises that it's up to her to look after ten year old James, nine year old Maybeth and six year old Sammy.

At first they stay close to the car, hoping their mother will come back, but by the second night they have attracted the attention of a security guard. Dicey, afraid that police intervention will see them separated into foster homes, decides they must find their own way to Bridgeport (home of the unknown relative), walking so as to save their few dollars for food. With the help of the road map they'd had in the car, she plots their route. They have now been on the road for several days and the money has all been used up, although Dicey has some lines and hooks given to her by a fisherman they'd talked to. Now in a beach camping area of a state park, they are marking time until James recovers from a bad fall. They'd spent part of the previous night with a couple of runaway teenagers, Edie and Louis. Reluctant to share any more information than is necessary, Dicey says her name is Danny. Anxious about James and about not being on the move, she wakes to another day . . .

DICEY AWOKE to the beginning of a bright day. She lay still for a long time, looking at the cloudless sky through the branches and leaves of green maples and sycamores. The leaves made designs on the background of the sky, intricate patterns that shifted with any slightest breeze. She heard James stir and rolled over on her side to watch him.

James' eyes opened. He yawned and stretched. Dicey waited for him to say what he always said first thing, about it still being true. Then everything would be back to normal.

He caught her eye. "I wish I'd seen you going into the boy's bathroom," he said. "I thought I'd split when Sammy told me."

"I noticed," Dicey said. "How's your head?"

James rolled it back and forth. "Almost OK," he said.

"What do you mean, almost? Does it hurt?"

James thought. "It feels tender. As if it could hurt. It doesn't exactly *hurt*, but it feels like it will."

Dicey sat up. "We can't go until James is better," she said sternly to herself, "that's the most important thing." So, they'd have to wait another day.

They had only apples left in their food supply, and Dicey wanted to save them, in case. So they went down to the little beach, leaving James behind. Three or four families already crowded the beach, and the Tillermans had to eat the apples for breakfast after all.

"It's a weekend," James explained. "That means a lot of people around, especially on the beaches, I bet."

"But what'll we do?" Dicey asked him. She answered herself. "We'll try fishing in the marsh. You'll have to stay here alone," she cautioned James.

"Danny?" a voice called from the road. "Is that you?" It was Edie, and Dicey stood up to show the girl where they were. Louis was with her. They had come, they said, to see how the third brother was and to warn the children that it was a weekend, so lots of people would be in the park.

Edie was carrying something bulky, an instrument. She sat down beside James and played on it a little, leaning it back against her shoulder. The sound was part banjo, part harp. "You like that?" she asked James.

"What is it?"

"An autoharp. Here," she said, and sang a song for them about a girl who wanted to follow her boyfriend to war.

"I like that," Maybeth said, when Edie finished.

"I do too, honey," Edie said. "Do you know any songs you'd like me to sing?" Maybeth shook her head.

Dicey looked at Edie over James' head and asked, "Do you know Pretty Peggy-O?"

"Sure," Edie said. She bent her head over the autoharp and her long hair fell down like a curtain. She strummed a couple of chords, then raised her face. But this wasn't their song. This song was about William the false lover and how he tricked pretty Peggy-O into running away with him but then murdered her. Edie sang the song quick and cruel, with sharp metallic sounds from her instrument.

"You're a good singer," James said.

"I thought we were going," Sammy said.

"Going where?" Edie asked.

"Fishing," Dicey told her.

"Do you have the hook and line?" James asked. Dicey nodded. "And worms?" She hadn't thought of bait. Count on James to think things through, Dicey thought, and forgave him for his lack of persistence the day before and for being careless and falling.

"Shall we stay with James?" Edie asked. Dicey didn't object.

When they had gotten out of earshot of the campsite, Sammy said he wasn't going fishing with them, he was going to the playground. He didn't want to walk any more, ever. He didn't want to explore. He wouldn't get into any trouble. He didn't mind being left alone. And he would not go with them, no matter what Dicey said or did.

Dicey decided she could probably leave him safely at the playground. She instructed him to go back to the campsite if he got bored, not to go wandering about. "And don't talk to anyone."

"Why not?" Sammy demanded.

"Well, you know, don't talk about us."

"I wouldn't do that. I'm not stupid."

Maybeth and Dicey crossed the dirt road from the playground and found the path to the small campground. Another path led to a bluff overlooking the marshes. They walked without speaking through the warm morning. The only sounds were the rustling of the leaves above them and the rustling of their feet on the leafy ground. They emerged from the woods on top of a low bluff that marked the border of the marshlands.

Below, the heavy grasses swayed. Narrow canals of water moved gently. The scene could have been painted in watercolors, so pale was the green of the grass, so subdued was the blue of the water.

They climbed down a short path and stood on the muddy ground of the lowlands. A heron looked up at them, curious but not afraid, before he flew to a more secluded spot. Clusters of gnats hovered in the air.

"It's so quiet," Dicey said. Maybeth nodded. "Think there are any fish?" Dicey asked, feeling her hunger. Maybeth didn't answer. Dicey walked out along the mudflat until she found a spot she liked. There she baited the hook with a worm from her pocket, put it into the water, and waited.

Maybeth sat beside her, braiding sea grass into long and useless lines. Dicey caught a fish almost right away, six or seven inches long. She rebaited the hook and caught another, even larger. She couldn't believe her luck. Every few minutes she could feel the tentative, jerking nibble on the end of her line.

When she had enough, Dicey took off her shirt and piled her catch into it. As long as they could fish, they wouldn't go hungry. She smiled at Maybeth. "Let's go back and eat," she said. It would be OK. They could wait for James to get well.

They stopped by the playground to pick up Sammy, but he wasn't there. Dicey hurried back to their camp. James sat alone, scratching at the ground with a stick. Fear clutched at Dicey's stomach. "Sammy?" she called. She shouldn't have left him alone for so long. "James, have you seen Sammy?"

Sammy stepped out from behind a boulder. Dicey let out a little snort of relief.

"Look." Dicey held up the fish she had caught. "Anybody hungry?"

"Why were you hiding?" Maybeth asked Sammy.

"We heard somebody coming. I didn't know who it was." His hazel eyes searched out Dicey's face, "I found something."

"What? Bring it over. We need some wood, too, to cook the fish."

Sammy went behind the boulder and came out holding a big grocery bag, which he set down before the fireplace. "Look at this," he said.

Egg salad sandwiches, a bag of potato chips, ham sandwiches, pieces of celery stuffed with peanut butter, a bag of cookies, paper plates, paper cups, paper napkins.

James sat silent, watching. "Where'd you find it?" Dicey asked.

"Left in the woods behind the bathrooms," Sammy said. "And some people gave me a hot dog too, but I ate it with them. They had catsup. I was so hungry," he said.

"Sammy," Dicey spoke slowly. "This looks like somebody's picnic."

"They might have forgotten it," Sammy said.

"That's not the truth," Dicey said.

"Is too," Sammy said.

"What's it matter?" James asked. "I mean, we're the hungry ones. They could probably go back to the store and buy food, whoever this belonged to. Or just go home and eat. We need it."

Dicey couldn't entirely disagree with him. "But it's stealing," she said.

"Just food," James argued. "Louis said it should be a natural right for everybody to have enough food."

"Does Louis know?"

"No. Sammy wasn't back."

"Sammy? Tell the truth," Dicey said.

"They left it on one of those tables. I don't know who they were. They left two bags on the table and I could see there was nobody watching, so I took one. I wanted you all to have something to eat. Dicey?" He made himself look straight at her. "I wanted to help out."

Dicey understood. "Well, you surely did that. But stealing — we don't steal." Not unless they had to, not unless they were starving, and then it should be Dicey herself to do it. Not a little boy six years old.

"I think it was pretty smart of him," James said. "And brave."

"I ran," Sammy boasted, "I ran so fast — it's hard to run with a big bag. Nobody caught me."

"I'm glad of that," Dicey said, reaching to pat his tangled hair. "I don't know how we would have gotten you back if you'd been caught."

"Would you get me back?" Sammy asked.

"Of course. What do you think?"

"I don't know," Sammy said.

"We're all together, aren't we?" Dicey asked him. "We'd just have to get you back. But it would be hard, really hard — so I'm glad."

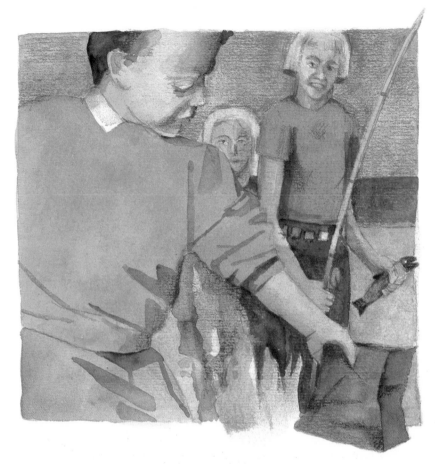

They ate the celery and the egg salad sandwiches right away, because mayonnaise could spoil. The rest of Sammy's food they put away for some other time. Meanwhile, they built a fire and roasted Dicey's fish over it. Even James was full when they finished. They stayed put for the rest of that long, early summer afternoon, but when the evening cool came into the air and the families on the beach left, the Tillermans went down by the water. James sat quietly by the water's edge, while the rest played tag until dark. James wanted quiet; the heat had given him a headache. But he told Dicey she didn't have to worry about him.

When they returned to the campsite, Louis and Edie were waiting for them. "James? We got you something," Edie said. "It's convalescent food." She handed him a small grocery bag. It held two oranges.

"Thanks," James said. "They look terrific." He peeled an orange and ate it.

Dicey grabbed the other one from him, peeled it and split it in half. She gave half to Maybeth and half to Sammy. James looked like he wanted to say something to her, but he didn't.

"Guess what?" Edie said. Her voice came out of the dark.

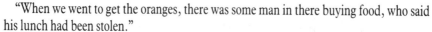

"What?"

"When we went to get the oranges, there was some man in there buying food, who said his lunch had been stolen."

Louis took over the story. "He was a big, fat guy. Asking what the country was coming to when a family's picnic lunch was stolen in a public park. He said it was probably dope addicts. He was all for calling in the police. But the guy who runs the store said it was probably somebody's idea of a joke. The big guy said that if he could get his hands on the joker, he'd show him what he thought of it. He reminded me of your father, didn't he, Edie? Isn't that just what your father would do? Then, he pulls out a wallet a foot thick, crammed with bills. He peels off a couple and goes out, still complaining about his bad luck. I say good luck to whoever walked off with his lunch."

"Why?" James asked.

"Big guys like that, with thick bankrolls — they've got so much that they don't know what to do with it. And they're always the first ones to call in the police on little guys. Like us. Like you."

Dicey went over to the trash barrel to throw out the orange peels. Edie went with her. "Danny? I wondered if you kids had taken it."

"No," Dicey said. "No, how could we? We were fishing at the marsh."

"I thought — you know — if you were hungry enough," Edie said.

"We're not hungry," Dicey said. "We've got plenty."

"If you say so," Edie said.

Louis called over, "Hey Danny, James says you caught a mess of fish."

Glad at the change of subject, Dicey told him about the marsh and how easy it was to catch fish there. Louis said it was illegal to fish in the marsh, because that area was a game sanctuary. "So you better be careful. You don't want to get caught at it."

How were they supposed to eat then, Dicey asked herself. By buying food, she answered. The whole world was arranged for people who had money — for *adults* who had money. The whole world was arranged against kids. Well, she could handle it. Somehow.

"If you were caught," Louis said. "Kids have no legal rights at all. That's one reason I took off. What about you kids, Danny? How come you're on the road?"

"Huh?" Dicey asked, pretending she hadn't been listening.

"You're about the most secretive bunch I've ever met," Louis said. "I don't even know where you're from. Where are you from?"

"Nowhere special," Dicey said.

"You don't trust me." Louis' voice hovered in the darkness. He waited for an answer.

"Don't tease him, Lou."

"I don't trust anyone," Dicey said. "It's what you said, kids have no rights. So we have to be extra careful."

"Why don't kids have any rights?" James asked.

"Because parents own them," Louis answered quickly. "Your parents can beat you, steal your money, decide not to take you to a doctor — anything they want."

"There's a law I have to go to school," James said. "That's a right isn't it?"

"If you look at it that way."

"They couldn't kill me," James continued. "That would be murder."

"If it could be proved."

James thought about this. "Then the only person who will look out for me is myself."

"You got it. And you better learn how to do that, learn quick and learn good. Look out for yourself and let the rest go hang — because they're out to hang you, you can be sure of it."

"What about love?" Edie asked.

"You tell us all about it, tell us all about your old man; and then talk about love," Louis said. "Danny here knows what's what — he doesn't trust anyone."

"What do you two do when you're not camping here?" Dicey asked them.

She saw the two heads turn towards one another, and the look they exchanged.

"I can't remember," Edie said, in a soft voice. "Nothing before now seems real to me any more. Nothing before is worth remembering."

"So I guess you'd say we didn't do anything. And now we do something — we pluck the lotus. Right, honey?"

Then they got up to leave. Edie said she'd come by tomorrow and bring James some soup. "That sounds good," James said. The two young people stole silently away. Dicey was listening, but she couldn't hear their footsteps. For a little while she wondered if they were hanging around, to overhear something.

The next morning, Sunday morning, dawned warm. Morning spread a haze of golden heat over the trees and boulders. James said it wasn't a good day for him to travel, it was too hot, it was too far, he just wasn't feeling right. So Dicey took her family across the top of the highland to the long beach. She guessed, correctly as it turned out, that that beach would be a favourite spot, that it would be crowded on this hot Sunday. She planned for the Tillermans to lose themselves among the mob of people there. James protested, saying he wanted to wait for Edie, but Dicey told him he had to come with them. The sun would give him a headache, he said. She said she thought he could stand that. "How much longer are we going to have to wait, anyway?" she demanded.

"I don't know. I told you, I'll say when I feel OK again," James said. "It's not my fault I'm sick."

Dicey didn't answer.

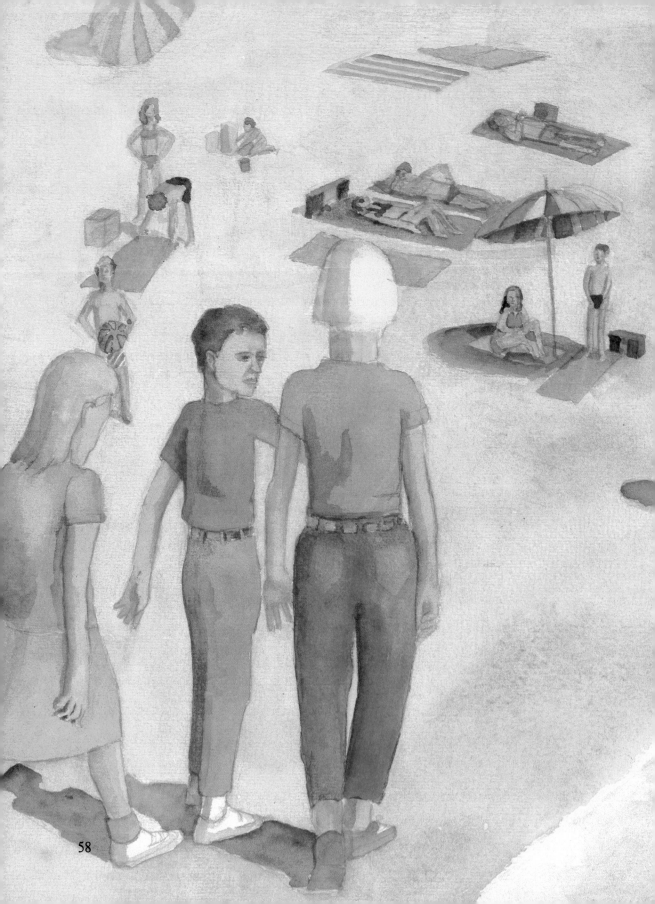

The long beach was a flat crescent that marked the edge of a shallow cove. Children straddled the water's edge and a few bolder ones were actually swimming. Towels crowded the sand, like bright pieces of confetti. On the towels lay people in bathing suits, surrounded by picnic baskets, paper bags, canvas totes, blaring radios and coolers full of ice and drinks.

The Tillermans walked about, unnoticed, and later returned to their camp for a quick lunch of ham sandwiches and potato chips, which finished off the food in Sammy's bag. Then they went back to the long beach. Dicey was glad not to meet Louis and Edie.

Later in the afternoon, when the beach began to empty, Dicey looked around, to gather James and Maybeth and Sammy together. They could leave tomorrow: she had watched James and she was pretty sure he was fine. Sammy was nowhere to be seen. Neither James nor Maybeth had spoken with him, not for a long time.

Dicey looked out over the low sandbars, not yet covered by the incoming tide. She knew she didn't have to worry about Sammy having drowned. She decided to wait a few minutes. He might, after all, just have slipped away to the woods to pee.

Sure enough, within ten minutes, she saw his sturdy body trudging down the path from the highlands. They went to meet him. As they walked along the cliff that fronted the Sound, Dicey asked him where he'd been. Sammy turned his head to look behind them, and then announced with swelling pride, "I got us another one".

"Another what?"

"Another food bag. It was all the leftovers a family couldn't finish. I watched them eat, then pack up the bag. Then they all went down to rinse off sand in the water, and I grabbed the bag, and I ran. It's at the camp."

"Good job, Sammy," James said.

"No it isn't," Dicey said. She knelt down in front of him. "And Sammy knows that," she said, looking straight in his eyes. His mouth grew stubborn and he would not look at her. "Stealing isn't right," Dicey said.

"Not even if you're hungry?" Sammy argued.

"You're not hungry, not really hungry," Dicey said. "We never stole things. Tillermans don't have to steal."

"Well, maybe we should," James interrupted. "It's like a war, isn't it? Us against everyone so we can get to Bridgeport. Otherwise, you'd have asked a policeman for help right away, when there was one hanging around our car. Remember?" Dicey remembered. "So if it's like that, what's wrong with Sammy taking somebody's leftovers?"

"And more too," Sammy grinned up at James. "There's money. A wallet."

"Oh no." Dicey groaned. "Sammy, you can't take a wallet the way you can food. You just can't get away with that. We have to take it back."

"No!" Sammy cried.

"Yes," Dicey said firmly. "And on the double. I'm right, aren't I, James?"

Even James agreed.

Dicey sent James and Maybeth on to gather mussels and clams and firewood. She hurried Sammy back to the camp, and he showed her where he'd hidden the stolen bag. "But they're gone home," he protested. "Their towel was gone when I came back."

Worse and worse, Dicey thought hard and fast. She took the wallet out of the bag — it was a man's wallet, brown leather — and grabbing Sammy by the hand, ran back to the long beach. She wanted to make him give it back himself and apologize. But she couldn't, not at the risk.

The long beach was empty under shadows that fell from the cliff out toward the water. But Dicey heard voices coming from somewhere. She stood halfway down the steep hill and made Sammy point to where he had found the bag. She lifted her arm and hurled the wallet at that spot. She didn't wait to see where it landed, but turned and ran back labouriously, uphill. She didn't wait for Sammy.

Safe again under cover of the trees, Sammy spoke sullenly, "It had almost twenty dollars in it".

Dicey didn't answer. She couldn't think of what to say. Finally she said, "You have got to do what I tell you. What *I* tell you, not anybody else."

Sammy nodded as if he understood.

They had a fire on the beach that evening and steamed mussels so hot and chewy they burned their tongues on the tawny meat. The smell of damp seaweed, richer than the smell of wet wood, rose with the smoke from the fire and lingered over their faces. They were salty after the day at the water. They were together. The light dimmed, melting into early twilight. Stars became visible, pinpricks of light on the silken sky. If they hadn't known better, they would have thought that when the fire died out and the moon shone bright in the sky, they could turn and trudge slowly up over familiar dunes to their own home. Where Momma would look up absentmindedly to greet them and ask if they had a good day.

Sammy dug wells for the water to run into. Maybeth arranged shells and water-polished stones into an intricate design. James skimmed rocks out over the water.

"We'll get going again tomorrow," Dicey said.

"I'm not sure, Dicey," James protested. "I don't think I should, yet." Dicey looked at him. He looked like he meant what he said.

"We could stay here," Sammy added. "It's OK here."

Dicey sat down beside the fire, her knees drawn up under her chin, poking at the blaze with a long stick and thinking. They had to go. But what if James wasn't better and it hurt him? Should she wait another day?

Louis and Edie came up silently behind her and surprised her with some chords on the autoharp. Dicey welcomed the music, but she had wanted to avoid any further contact with them.

Edie played and sang. Louis took Maybeth by the hand and led her in a galloping dance up and down the beach. Sammy trailed them in a jig of his own, while James clapped time energetically. Dicey watched him — some brother! He was no more sick than she was. They were leaving tomorrow, if she had to drag them out of the park herself.

The dance over, they all relaxed around the fire while Edie continued to sing. Louis held Maybeth at his side. Sammy curled up against Dicey. The sky turned black velvet. Deep satin water curled against the sand.

"We gotta go to sleep," Dicey said, after a while.

"Don't go yet, Danny," Edie said, putting down the autoharp. "I don't know when I've had a better time."

Dicey stood up and dusted sand from her jeans. Barely awake, Sammy waited beside her. James stayed seated, his eyes reproachful.

"Maybeth?" Dicey spoke gently.

Maybeth came over.

"Goodnight, honey," Louis said.

Maybeth didn't answer.

"Doesn't she ever say anything?" Louis asked.

"Sure. Sometimes."

"Wait," Edie said, "we'll come with you."

They climbed up the step path. At the top of the hill, Dicey turned to say good night, so they would go away, but Louis was holding onto Edie's arm and pointing.

Between the trees they saw a bright light that rhythmically flashed red.

"What is it?" Dicey asked.

"Shut up," Louis said. "Move it, Edie." They slipped away into the darkness.

He was right, Dicey realised. It was a police car going along the road that ran past the campsites. She pulled her family into the bushes and told them to lie down.

"It's a police car," James said quietly. "Heading towards our camp."

"I dumped the bag in the trash," Dicey said.

"That's where they'll look," James said.

"I can't see what's going on," Dicey said. "Lie quiet, everyone."

Darkness rustled through the trees. Faintly, the water lapped at the shore. Dicey thought. "We're going up to the woods past the playground, long way around," she said. "We'll sleep there and get out of here at first morning."

"But . . ." James said.

Dicey felt Maybeth's small hand on her arm. "But nothing. You've been fine all day today, and you know it. Don't lie to me, not any more. I won't believe you."

They waited a long time, then began a silent journey across the dark park. They made a wide circle around their campsite. They saw nothing, they heard nothing, only the insects and the noise of the wind. Dicey was sure of her direction, but she wasn't sure just where they were until she saw the pale emptiness of the playground before her. They were so tired by then that they just stumbled into the woods beyond and slept there, slept uneasily.

by Cynthia Voigt
Illustrated by Joh Canty

Away from Home

You can be away from home for lots of reasons. This is what it was like for some fourth year pupils at two schools in Bristol. The schools are Elmlea Junior School and Shirehampton Junior School.

A couple of years ago I went on a surprise holiday to Florida in America. We left home at about three o'clock in the morning. We had to go on a coach to Heathrow Airport for two and a half hours. When we got to Heathrow it was cold and the plane was delayed for an hour. I was starving and bored so I stuffed myself with chocolate. Then we got on the plane, my ears kept popping.

When we got to Bermuda we stayed there for a while and then carried on to Orlando. We stayed there for three days and then we went to a hotel in Disney World. The first day we went to Disney World it was boiling hot and that day and the next day we went on all the rides in the Magic Kingdom. The next two days we spent in the Epcot Centre. There was this thing like a huge golf-ball. You went inside and you were taken on a ride up, round and everywhere on a sort of slow roller-coaster, from the past to the present and on to the future. Disney World is full of big moving models of people and things. You can get around Disney World on this sort of train thing which runs on a rail high up in the air. One of the routes took you right through a hotel with people in it! We also went on the cable car which takes you all round the Magic Kingdom.

We went back to the hotel by the Atlantic in Cocoa Beach for nine days. The sea was dark blue like the pen I write with. My feet were boiling when I got onto the sand and there were loads of jellyfish on the beach. After you got out of the sea you washed yourself in the showers. The water was freezing cold.

Just before we went home we went to Cape Kennedy and we saw one of the rockets.

Michael Budd

"Bye mum, see you tomorrow" (I hope!)
I'm missing mum and dad already.
Time for bed...
Oh no, not
The dreaded SLEEPING BAG!
This room is nothing like my cosy little room,
The place is eerie, the walls are damp,
I've got an empty feeling inside,
There is no carpet, the floor is cold,
The bed isn't as comfortable as my bed,
I still miss my parents.
I hope I survive the night!

Andrew Chappell.

When I stay overnight at my friend's house I find it a mixture of excitement and the jitters. We stay up late because it's usually a Saturday and there's no school next day. We plan midnight feasts but we never have them because 1) we fall asleep or 2) we can't stay up that long and so we eat it before midnight!
Abbie McCartney

I'm going to camp tomorrow. I don't really like it but mum says I've got to go or it's a waste of money. I hate leaving home, leaving mum and dad. I hate leaving my lovely warm bed.
    Well... "Bye mum, bye dad!"
    I hear mum in the background saying "You haven't forgotten your toothpaste, have you?
    "No, mum," I shout.
    It's night-time now. I've got to sleep in that horrible, cold, damp tent and all I've got to keep me warm is my sleeping bag.
    In the night I feel splashing water on my head. It's a hole in the tent. I'll have to block it with my sock.
    Then the morning came. My sock was all damp so I had to walk round with a wet sock.

Jonathan Barnes

I pack my bags and get ready to go to gran's. I say goodbye to mum and dad and give them a kiss. We arrive at gran's, it's nearly time to go to bed. The bed that I have to sleep in is not as nice as my own. I miss mum and dad a lot and I wish I was at home. Gran wakes me up and I have a lovely cooked breakfast. Then Gran says we might go to the beach! I'm starting to enjoy it!

Jenna Palmer

My family told me it would only be for a week.
"It's for your own good," they said.
Were they right? Or were they wrong?
I guess I'll never know.

They sent me to this place, like hell it was.
Day after day,
Week after week, I stayed there.
They lied to me!
They cheated me!
My own family!
I'm going to be here for eternity, eternity.

Chris Phyo

Sometimes when I'm all alone,
It feels as if the world's closed down
There's no-one there to talk to or play with,
No-one there to comfort or care for me.
I keep on thinking, "Where's everybody gone?"

Mark Beese

On the 23rd of October I went out to play and I fell over. I banged my head. It was a bit sore at first and I felt dizzy. I went home and I felt a bit sick. I fell asleep for a few hours and when I woke up I was dizzy again. I had some tea but then I was sick so my mum phoned the hospital. She told them what had happened and they said "Bring your son up to the hospital."

I went to the toilet and my mum got my stuff. My dad washed out the bowl that I was sick in and my mum wrapped me up warm.

When I got to the hospital I was very hot and I felt sick. The nurse told me to change into my pyjamas and get into bed. Then she took me to the X-ray room. On the door it had a radiation sign and I thought I was going to die of radiation! They took an X-ray of a third of my brain. It was OK but they said I had to stay in the night. I felt weird and funny. They put me in an ambulance and took me over to the children's ward.

They put me into bed and the nurse looked at me to see if I was OK. I didn't feel sick any more, I felt tired so I went to sleep and my mum and dad went home. I woke up and the doctor was there. I felt scared because I hadn't seen him before. Then I went into the playroom and I had my breakfast.

The nurse said, "Do you want a lot of milk or a little bit of milk?" I said I wanted a lot. She gave me half a centimetre in the bottom and the Weetabix was dry. I had a sore on the side of my mouth and I had a whacking great spoon. I couldn't get the spoon in my mouth. I felt hungry.

When I was in the playroom a lady came out of the school room and said I had to go in there with the rest of the kids. I felt silly in the school room because I was in my pyjamas.

Then my mum came and we went home. I was glad to be back.

Daniel Managh

UP THE PIER

Mr Pontifex looked surprised when Carrie came down to the pier again that day. Straight after tea she raced down towards the sea, knowing that there was only an hour or two of daylight left. Already she was familiar with the way, had made a small corner of Llangolly her own.

The gatekeeper was even more surprised when Carrie asked for a season ticket.

"Season?" he echoed. "The season's over, missy."

"I mean the *winter* season," she said firmly. She had half expected this. She felt certain that there was some mysterious link between him and the dog and boy. Why else should he have pretended not to have seen them?

"Staying long, then?" he asked, rummaging in his drawer.

"I don't know," she replied truthfully. "I may be, and I may not."

"Shouldn't have thought there was much on a pier for a young 'un, this time of year," he went on. "If it's slot machines you're after, there's an arcade in the Queen's Road."

"Oh, it's not the slot machines," Carrie said. "I didn't even notice there were any. You know that kiosk on the left, the first one along?"

He looked up.

"Has it been empty long?"

"All summer," he said. "Piers ain't what they were, these days. There's not the same call for them."

Carrie was hardly listening. She was thinking, "Empty all summer, yet the newspapers were put over the windows in the last day or two. Why?"

"Ah, when I was a lad, that was the days for piers," went on the old man. "Fifty year ago and more, a pier was a pier then. Like a world of its own, it was. I come of a pier family, you know. The day was when Llangolly pier was Pontifex from top to bottom, as you might say."

He sighed.

"There's a mad fool I was, when I was young. Ran off to sea when I was but fifteen. Gone twenty year and more I was, all told. And when I come back —"

He spread his fingers and shrugged.

"What?"

"Gone. All of 'em. As I might have knowed they'd be, I s'pose. Always on the move, pier folk."

"Oh! How terrible!" Carrie cried. "And did you never find them?"

"Never, missy. Didn't try. I'd run off from 'em, see, and hardly liked to face 'em. Only lately I've thought of 'em much at all. Must be getting old — dreaming about the old days. Fifty year and not so much as a whisper of 'em, then —"

He broke off suddenly.

"Here we are. Don't lose it." He pushed the ticket towards her over the counter. "Not going down tonight, are you?"

She nodded.

"Lights don't go on," he warned. "Not after September 30th. Don't you get left down there in the dark."

"I won't," she said.

She began to walk rapidly away, eager to reach the wooden deck, the *real* pier. A slow autumn dusk was already gathering and the line between sea and sky was blurred on the horizon. The gulls were quiet now, the clamour of the morning forgotten. She noticed that only an odd one here and there smoothly rode the quiet evening air, *swam* in it, as if it were deep water.

Carrie's pace slackened. All at once she felt that she had been mistaken, that there *was* no mystery, that the pier was as empty as it seemed to be, shuttered against the coming of the winter. None the less, something seemed to draw her on, and looking down she saw that she had already reached the line where wood and tarmac met.

Playing an old, childish game, she kept her eyes fixed downwards and began to tread the boards in a ritual pattern. She carefully stepped with the ball of her foot each time on every third plank, tiptoeing to keep her foot clear of the others as if her life depended on it. But the planks were narrow and her balance unsteady, and after the first few steps she felt herself swaying and threw out her arms to balance herself. In vain. Her foot missed the allotted plank and the rhythm was broken.

She lifted her head and saw for the first time that she was not alone. A little group of figures stood by the first kiosk, the empty one, and a dog sat watching close by. She stared at them and they stared back, and as their gazes met and locked, part of her mind was suddenly aware that one of the figures was the boy she had met on the beach, and another part was that the seagulls had been thrown into panic again. All in a moment they had come crowding from their hideouts in the Strindel and set up a coarse, deafening clamour right above Carrie's head, throwing her into a kind of daze.

Then she saw that the watching faces had changed now, they wore expressions of bewilderment, even alarm, and the man and the woman exchanged uneasy glances.

"George," said the young woman in a low voice, "she ain't *seeing* us, surely?"

"Seems to." The man gave Carrie another hard look. "Straight at us, she's looking. I could swear she's seeing us."

"What's gone wrong?" wailed the woman then. "What'll we do?"

"Hold steady, Ellen," the man said. "Wait. See what happens."

Carrie shifted her gaze back to the boy. He too stood watching, wordless and alert. She suddenly knew that they might stand there for ever, all four of them, locked in an endless stare, unless she herself made the first move. They were waiting for *her*.

"Hello," she heard her own voice croak, and it sounded so hoarse and far away, so lost amid the shrieking of the gulls, that she cleared her throat and said it again, "Hello!", so loudly this time that it came out as a shout.

"She *do* see us!" cried the woman then, and clutched at the man's sleeve. "Oh — whatever? What'll we do?"

"It's the same one, pa," the boy said then. "The one who was down this morning, remember? The one on the beach I told you about. She's on to us, pa! Must be!"

Looking into those three faces, frightened and aghast, became almost unbearable. They were looking at her as if she were some kind of monster. Pleadingly she stretched out a hand.

"What's wrong?" she cried. "What have I done?"

They did not answer. If anything, she seemed to have made matters worse.

"She sees us *and* hears us," said the man, and his voice was not quite steady. "But it's not the end of things. Just keep calm, and act natural."

He, too, cleared his throat.

"Evening," he said, and this time he was speaking direct to Carrie.

"Good evening!" she cried, weak with relief, feeling human again.

"There you are," said the man to the woman. "Answers straight back, you see."

"Why does he keep talking as if I'm not here?" wondered Carrie desperately. "What's *happening*?"

"If we act natural, we might win through yet," the man went on. "You say something to her" — nudging the boy.

"Had a good paddle this afternoon, did you?" asked the boy obediently.

"O yes, thank you!" Carrie cried.

"Me and Muff went rock climbing," he went on.

"We was just having a last stroll down the pier," the man put in quickly, frowning at the boy as if to warn him not to say too much.

"N-nice evening for a stroll," the woman managed.

"Lovely," agreed Carrie warmly. She heard the tremor in the voice, and willed the woman not to be afraid of her.

"It's lovely," she said again.

Just then the dog rose, stretched, and padded towards Carrie. He sniffed and wagged his tail and Carrie, grateful for at least this show of friendship, bent and patted his head.

"Good dog, Muff," she said, and now her voice trembled, too.

"We'll be getting along, then," said the man. He took the woman's arm firmly and motioned to the boy with his head. "'Night, missy."

"Oh — good-bye!" Carrie cried. Were they really going? And where? All she could do herself now was begin to walk away from them, up the pier. After a few yards she turned and looked back. They were all still standing there in a close-knit group, watching. Hastily the man threw up a hand in a half-wave, pulled at the woman's arm and began walking determinedly in the opposite direction. The boy gave her a final, curious stare, and followed suit.

After that, Carrie dared not look back again. Already they saw her as someone dangerous, perhaps as a spy.

"But why?" she thought, and found herself saying the words out loud. "Why?"

Then, too, there was the strange witness of the gulls. *They* knew that something mysterious was afoot on Llangolly pier. She could still hear their clamour following after.

Right to the very end of the pier she walked, into the gathering dusk, and stood watching the tiny lights of ships far out on the sea's rim. There she went over the encounter in her mind, looking for clues.

Oddly enough, now that she could no longer actually *see* the trio, she was more aware of their appearance. There had been something strange about them, even apart from their hard gaze and pale, frightened faces. Something . . . something that she could hardly place — was it to do with the clothes they were wearing? Try as she might, she could not remember their costume except as a vague impression — it was the faces she could still see in her mind's eye, and the watchful eyes. But the longer she thought, the more she felt certain that there *had* been something odd about their dress, something vaguely old-fashioned and out of date.

Now the light had nearly gone and Carrie remembered that she had promised to be back at Craig Lea before dark. She set back towards land at a run. As she ran she could see a few lights here and there along the margin of the bay, but the pier itself, as Mr Pontifex had warned her, was in darkness. The festoons of fairylights hung dead and dark as stones between the lamp-posts.

She did not pause for breath until she reached the first pair of kiosks, and then she halted for a moment, hearing her own breathing and the regular rise and fall of the waves below. The gulls had evidently screeched themselves into silence and taken off to their perches in the Strindel. The little kiosks stood blank and shuttered.

Of the strange trio there was not a sign. They had vanished. Of that, Carrie felt certain. Wherever they had gone, they had simply vanished.

She went on walking. As she left the dock behind and set foot on land again, a single, solitary gull perched on the railings let out a shrill, startled cry and flew up, circling overhead and rousing answering cries from the near-by rocks.

Scared by the harsh cry out of the dark Carrie began to run again. The gull followed, scolding noisily. Only as she pushed through the turnstile and stood panting on the promenade did it make a final, wheeling dive and fly off, merging into the gloom.

Carrie stared after it, and as she stood there, suddenly felt that she was being watched. She turned towards the little stone gatehouse and for a fraction of a second was certain that she saw the curtains at the lighted window stir and settle, as if somebody had been peering between them . . .

She began to run again, this time not stopping till she reached the bottom of the stone steps outside the hotel. Craig Lea might not be home, but at least it was safety . . .

The smell that rose from under the pier was strong and cold, a wet-stone, wet-weed, wet-sand smell. It was a smell of age and yet fresh and salty, and to Carrie it was beginning to be the smell of excitement. By ten o'clock, just as the morning mist was dissolving and the heavy dew drying, she was back on the still damp boards, eyes fixed on that first white kiosk and its blank, newspapered windows.

She sniffed in the cold air gladly, ridding her nostrils of the smell of dust and wax polish and who-knows-what-scented air-fresheners that hung in the high, silent rooms of Craig Lea. She had earned her freedom that day, had dusted the empty bedrooms, mopped their cold brown lino and run to the grocers and back twice for Aunt Pester. (She had decided that this was how she would think of her aunt in her own mind. It put her at a satisfying distance — in her place, in fact.)

So virtuous did she feel, so deserving of reward, that it was with a curious sense of flatness that she stood now staring at the spot where she had expected to find *something* — what, she did not know. Even the gulls were in workaday mood — diving, flying, sitting on rails, their world intact and unalarmed. It was a plain, peaceful October morning with everything in its right place, and Carrie felt betrayed.

She crossed to the other kiosk, the one with the photographs, and gazed at the old summer scenes. The pictures on the door caught her eye again, and something about them made her look more closely. 'Llangolly Pier Fifty Years Ago' a caption read. But it was a strange familiarity about the pictures themselves that held her, though at first it eluded her, maddeningly, like a half-forgotten tune. She stared at the brownish prints of thin ladies in tube dresses, moustached men and poker-faced children, straining to capture the mislaid likeness. And when it came it was in a flash, and she let out a cry of recognition.

It was the clothes! That was it — that was what she had half known the night before — that strange, frightened trio she had met only a few yards from where she was standing now — these were the clothes they had been wearing! She was certain of it — she could see again the silhouette of the woman, long and narrow, and of the man's trousers, caught in below the knee like plus-fours. He had even worn a moustache!

At that very moment, as if in sympathy, the gulls went into storm again, but by now Carrie was past noticing. Her eye had fallen on one particular print, right on the bottom row, in the middle. Three figures stared solemnly back at her as they had stared into the camera lens half a century ago. A man, a woman and a boy. *Them.*

Carrie let out a long, gasping breath.

"Hello," said a voice behind her.

She whirled round. It was the boy. He wore a ring of angry gulls like a halo. She stared into his unmistakably live face, speechless. He had stepped out of that sepia print, flesh and blood, and was now regarding her with a long, curious stare for all the world as if it were *she* who was the ghost.

Written by Helen Cresswell
Illustrated by Liz Anelli

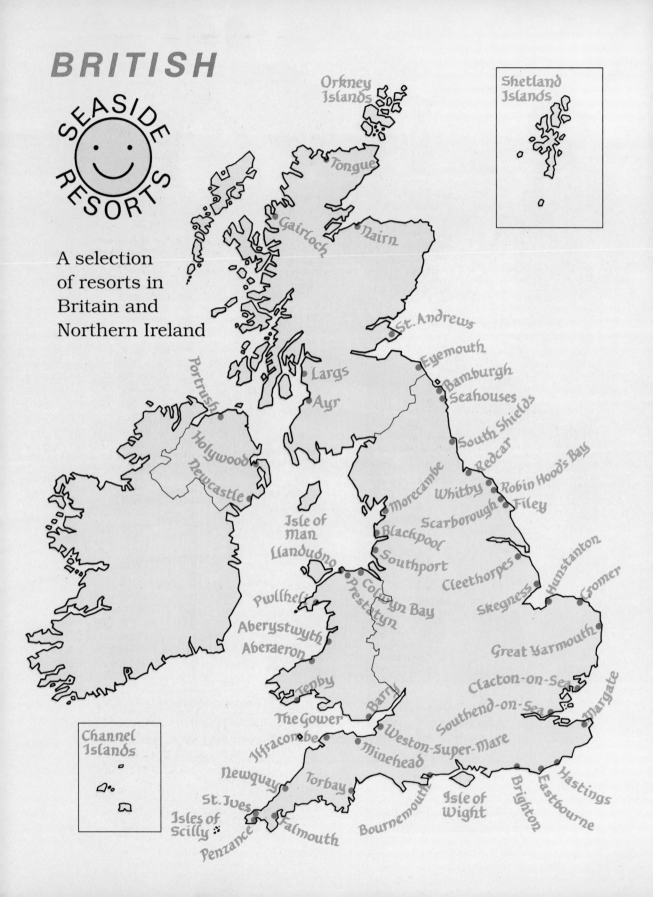

BRITISH

SEASIDE RESORTS

A selection
of resorts in
Britain and
Northern Ireland

Shetland
Islands

Orkney
Islands

Tongue

Gairloch

Nairn

St. Andrews

Eyemouth

Largs

Bamburgh

Ayr

Seahouses

Portrush

South Shields

Holywood

Redcar

Newcastle

Morecambe

Whitby

Robin Hood's Bay

Isle of
Man

Scarborough

Filey

Llandudno

Blackpool

Southport

Cleethorpes

Hunstanton

Pwllheli

Colwyn Bay

Cromer

Prestatyn

Skegness

Aberystwyth

Great Yarmouth

Aberaeron

Clacton-on-Sea

Tenby

Margate

Barry

Southend-on-Sea

The Gower

Weston-Super-Mare

Ilfracombe

Minehead

Newquay

Torbay

Hastings

Bournemouth

Isle of
Wight

Brighton

Eastbourne

Channel
Islands

St. Ives

Falmouth

Isles of
Scilly

Penzance

Promenade, Blackpool

Whalebone Arch, Whitby

The beach, Portrush

Brighton beach and pier

Tenby Harbour

St. Michael's Mount, Cornwall

Why the Sea is Salt

a Norwegian Folktale

He put the mill on the table and told it first to grind candles, then meat, then ale, then bread, until they had everything that was nice for Christmas fare.

They ground out enough meat and drink to last until Twelfth Day and on the third day they asked all their friends and relatives to a feast. The older brother was green with envy when he discovered it had all come from the magic mill.

He set his heart on owning the mill and he nagged and he chaffered and he haggled until at last the younger brother agreed to sell it to him for three hundred gold coins, but he took good care not to tell him how the mill worked.

Next morning the older brother sent his wife out to watch the mowers cut the hay. When dinner time came round he put the mill on the kitchen table.

The mill began to grind....

and grind...

... and grind, but the older brother did not know how to stop it. Soon the house was full of herrings and broth. They began to pour out of the doors and windows. He snatched up the mill and ran for his life.

Help! Help!

Run for your lives before we're all drowning in broth!

Down the road he ran with the stream of herrings and broth roaring like a waterfall over the whole farm.

OPERATION ASTERIX

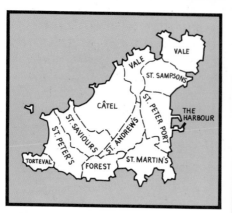

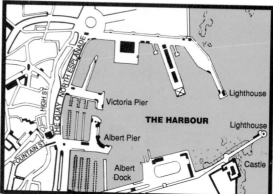

It was Christmas Day 1982 and Richard Keen, a diver and fisherman, was diving for scallops in the harbour of St Peter Port, Guernsey. Christmas Day is the only day in the year when diving in the harbour is permitted. As he was swimming through the icy water in the entrance to the harbour, he saw what he thought was the wreck of an eighteenth century ship.

Next Christmas he dived to the wreck once more. Some of the timbers had moved and he found a Roman tile and a Roman coin. The wreck was obviously much older than he had first thought. Richard Keen contacted his friend Dr Margaret Rule, the archeologist who had been involved in the raising of the *Mary Rose*.

St Peter Port is a very busy harbour which is used by cross-Channel ferries. The wash from the propellers of the ferries had been responsible for partly uncovering the wreck. In a short time they would destroy it as they passed above. So began the first underwater rescue excavation ever carried out in Britain. As Margaret Rule said during the BBC television programme about the wreck: "We had to save her, record her and begin to understand her."

Operation Asterix was a race against time which began in 1984 with the setting up of The Guernsey Maritime Trust. It wasn't going to be easy. The water temperature was about seven degrees centigrade, each diver could only work a maximum of two hours underwater and for two shifts a day. Work would have to stop completely and the divers and boat move away every time a ferry came in or out of the harbour.

The actual work began on November 4th. A steel framework was erected over the wreck so that the divers could lean on it and only touch the wreck with their hands. A water-driven vacuum cleaner was used to clear away the lighter sand and sediment. Every time that work stopped for a ferry (about four times a day) more sand would be stirred up. Before they could carry on each time, the new sand and sediment had to be sucked away. Then something interesting emerged: a layer of solidified pitch nearly six metres square covered a large part of the wreck.

In this pitch were bits of pottery and debris, all fused together. It would need to be removed, bit by bit, and carefully taken ashore for analysis. The pitch and its contents provided evidence of the ship's date, cargo and origins. It also proved that the ship had sunk because of a fire on board — the fire had melted the pitch. No human remains were found and, because the ship sank so close to the harbour and so close to the end of its voyage, we can assume that the crew survived the sinking.

Operation Asterix vessels moored above the dive team, 1985

On November 16th the first of the ship's timbers were removed and taken ashore. This was done by a method which had been learned during the *Mary Rose* investigation. The body of a lorry was cut off; it was then loaded under the water and hauled up again. The timbers were wrapped in plastic and then put in shallow tanks of water ashore to keep them wet until they could be properly preserved.

Pressed by time, the divers worked into the night with underwater lights. The team knew that it would be impossible to record the position of every timber in the ship and then bring them all ashore in the time that was left before the Autumn gales and tides came. After the rough winter weather would come the big spring tides and what was left of the wreck could be lost forever. So the last part of the November diving period was spent in placing sixteen tons of sandbags over the wreck for protection. On November 20th the wreck was left to face the winter storms.

Diver preparing timbers for removal

On April 9th 1985 the work started again — just two weeks before the huge spring tide which would finish off anything that was then left. The water was even colder than it had been in the autumn and the variations in the tides were enormous — a good ten metres or so. At low water the propellers of the ferries passed only two metres above the wreck.

Two divers working on the wreck. One has an underwater notepad, the other has polythene boxes to collect samples

A grid of strings in ten centimetre squares was placed over the wreck to help make the painstaking work of recording by photograph and drawing more accurate. It had to be done by looking straight down onto the wreck and not from an angle and the grid helped the divers to check this. The record of where everything was placed was essential if any reconstruction of the ship was to be made.

By April 21st the work was completed: the timbers were ashore and the spring tides could do their worst. The emergency part of *Operation Asterix* was over and the analysis and reconstruction of the ship could continue without the race against time.

Why is this wreck so important?

There have been many examples of Roman wrecks found in the Mediterranean Sea but the Guernsey wreck is different. It dates from the later part of the second century and was built in the style of Celtic ships — very few of these remains have ever been found. The timbers of the ship are oak and there are no fastenings between the outer planks. There were fixed to the framework with heavy iron nails which, of course, had rusted away completely having been underwater for about 1700 years.

The keel planks

The evidence from the wreck suggests that the ship was a sailing ship with one mast. It was flat-bottomed and between twenty and twenty-five metres long. The hearth from the ship's galley where food was cooked was found — broken into many small pieces. Over the top of the hearth there would have been a small roof made of standard Roman roof tiles. Two of the remains of these tiles have the imprints of dog's paws on them!

Over 2,000 finds had been trapped in the layer of pitch which had melted over the stern of the ship. These included grains of wheat and seeds which provided evidence of where the ship had come from. Other finds from the ship include belt buckles, fish hooks, brooches and ship's fittings such as small sail rings made of rope.

A group of third century coins found in the ship

Part of a pottery bowl found in the crew's quarters

Tile fragment with animal paw print

Operation Asterix was unique. The race against time by a group of dedicated divers and archaeologists has given us the most complete example of this type of ship ever found. It is also the oldest sea-going ship ever discovered outside the Mediterranean. The treasure from *Operation Asterix* has not been gold or silver, but new knowledge and information.

95

Diary of an Emigrant

JOURNEY TO AUSTRALIA IN THE YEAR 1883

*Some years ago my mother gave me
an old diary. The diary was written by
my great uncle, William Collis and it
describes his journey to Australia in 1883.
Will was twenty at the time and his brother,
Caleb, who went with him, was twenty-three.
Travelling to Australia over a hundred years
ago was nothing like travelling to Australia
today! The extracts which you are about
to read are just as my great uncle Will
wrote them so long ago . . .*

Wendy Body

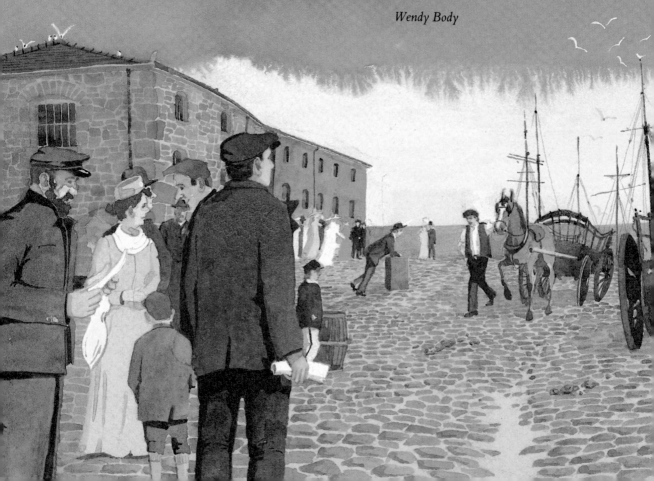

On the morning of September 6th 1883 we departed from home for Plymouth, en route for New South Wales, Australia. We arrived at the depot at 5.30 p.m., and on showing our papers to the gatekeeper, he admitted us. He then proceeded to tell us to understand that we would not be allowed out again until we went on board the *S. S. Sydenham*. The emigration depot is composed of four blocks of buildings. They are built mainly of stone, and were formerly used as barracks during the time of the Russian war.

One block is used for the single girls, one for the single men, one for the married persons, and the other building is used partly as a luggage room, and the other part as the Depot Master's residence. The building has a large yard in front of it which faces the water.

We found plenty of company in the yard, there being 369 emigrants for the *S. S. Rialto* and 342 including ourselves for the *S. S. Sydenham*. At six o'clock a bell rang, summoning us for tea. The single men and married people messed together and on entering the mess room, we were greeted with some nice music! Children were screaming, men whistling, women shouting and all intermixed with the jingle of the crockery-ware.

We seated ourselves at a table with some more fresh arrivals. Presently a sprightly man called "Old John" came and stood at the head of our table and said,

"Now listen to what I have got to say: what I have got to say is this: we have no gentlemen's sons here, all that comes here, has to do his fair share of work. You will sit ten to a table, you must also appoint a Captain to take charge of your mess, to see that your food is equally divided, and table, forms and crockery

kept clean. The Captain must appoint two persons each day to wash up after meals."

After he had given us our instructions he blew a whistle, "Silence," he said, then started to distribute tickets to each mess, which were to be delivered up at the Kitchen for tea. Each mess was allowed a large pot of tea, five pounds of bread, and a small dish of butter.

We amused ourselves in the evening watching the boats on the water until it was quite dark, after which there was some singing, music, and dancing in the wash house.

At 9 p.m. the bell rang for bedtime, we were conducted to our sleeping apartment by Old John, who blew his whistle and said,

"Now listen to what I got to say, what I got to say is this; there is no convenience upstairs, so if anyone wants to go down in the night, take your boots in your hands, and don't make a noise."

Two men were appointed to see that we all got into bed quietly and also to put the lights out. In our room there were sixty beds, thirty each side, one row about six inches above the floor, and another two feet above that, each bunk being seven feet long and two feet wide.

As soon as the lights were extinguished, some amusing games began as you may suppose. When sixty young men are in one room there is sure to be some fun, in fact, sleep was out of the question for two to three hours. The next evening, our luggage was brought from Devonport railway station to the depot free of charge, then duly examined by a female inspector to see if we carried firearms or any combustibles, and also to see if we had the required clothing. We had to buy some yellow soap and some marine soap.

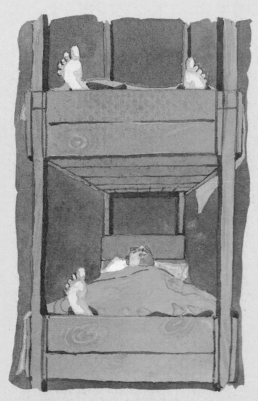

Friday Sept. 7th

At six o'clock in the morning, we were all aroused by the bell, it wasn't long before Old John appeared and shouted,

"Now you young men for Australia show a leg, show a leg, show a leg."

At the same time he hauled out all the reluctant ones. John had been a man-of-wars man, he was not to be trifled with. As soon as we were dressed, John made us all fold our sheets and blankets and place them in uniform style at the foot of our bunks, after which we made a concerted rush for the wash house, there being a limited supply of washing bowls, and no end to the great unwashed. However, after clinging to a bowl for half an hour or so, we would manage to get a lick if not a kick.

After having washed we then amused ourselves watching fishing smacks coming in until breakfast time. The fishermen would often throw us a few mackerel. I managed to get one in the scramble and had it for tea. At eight o'clock the bell rang for breakfast. We had the same amount of food as we had for tea the night before — if we wanted any extra we could get it on the premises, there being a store kept by the depot master.

The S. S. *Rialto* emigrants left this morning by a small steamer, and went on board about a mile out in the harbour, we gave them some hearty cheers as they moved off and wished them bon voyage. We had learned earlier that a Mr Cole had been appointed constable on the *Rialto* for which he would receive three pounds at the end of the voyage.

We dined at 1 p.m. the bill of fare, roast beef, and boiled potatoes — the Roman Catholics having potatoes and butter, their creed not allowing them to eat meat on Fridays. However, they all got together and complained to their priest in the evening and he then gave them permission to eat meat on the voyage.

A Church of England clergyman delivered a sermon to us in the evening, giving us some very good advice; he likened Australia to the land flowing with milk and honey. He also gave us some tracts and books which he said we could read on the voyage.

After the sermon, we had some fiddling and dancing in the yard until bedtime. After a little while Old John appeared, he said he would give us the cream of it tonight, so he did. He put us in a thickly populated and more noisy bedroom than last night, little did he know that we thought "the more the merrier". After a good game of leap frog, and sundry other games, we sank in sweet repose until the morning, when we were woken by Old John and the bell at 6 a.m.

Saturday Sept. 8th

The *S. S. Rialto* set sail this morning at 5 a.m. The *S. S. Sydenham* is not in yet, we are all anxiously watching for her arrival.

In the afternoon we were served out with our ship's kit which consisted of two canvas bags to put our clothes in, knife and fork, two spoons (one tea and one dessert), tin plate and tin mug for each person; three tea pots, two coffee pots, meat, soup, and vegetable tin, two tea caddies, two coffee tins, one butter tin, two sugar tins, one pepper box, one mustard pot and two meat nets for each mess, eight to a mess on the vessel. We also received a card with the number of our bunk in the vessel, my number being ninety-two and my brother ninety, next door on the same floor.

In the evening we were amused by a party of Irish people, singing their national songs in the washhouse.

Sunday Sept. 9th

While we were having breakfast this morning, Old John came in, blew his whistle and ordered silence and began thus:

"Now listen to what I have got to say, what I have got to say is this: the doctor has given orders that as soon as you have breakfasted and cleaned up your tea things, you can go out for three hours until 12 o'clock."

When we heard this good news, we cheered Old John until he was glad to clear out.

We all went out about 9 a.m. and had a good walk through the town until church time, when some of us went to church. We went back to the depot at 12 o'clock and as soon as dinner was over we were allowed out again until 4 p.m. In the evening we had some sacred songs sung in the yard, which made it seem more like the Sabbath day.

Monday Sept. 10th

We were allowed out today, the same hours as yesterday. It was wet and very miserable walking about. We bought some cheese biscuits and preserved meat to take with us on the voyage.

Six hundred and sixty-three fresh faces in the depot tonight, they are emigrants bound for Queensland by the steamship *Duke of Beaucleaugh* which leaves Plymouth tomorrow the eleventh of September 1883.

Tuesday Sept. 11th

We were allowed out today same as before. We saw the wreck of a Norwegian barge which was wrecked Sunday September 2nd on the rocks at Plymouth Hoe. Her crew, seven in number, were all saved by the lifeboat crew.

The Duke Of Beaucleaugh left Plymouth harbour about 3 p.m. this afternoon with six hundred and sixty-three emigrants and twenty-two passengers from London, bound for Queensland.

Wednesday Sept. 12th

We were allowed out today for only one hour, from ten till eleven a.m.

No tidings of the *S. S. Sydenham*; a tug is sent out about eleven miles twice every day to bring her in the harbour as soon as she is sighted. All busy this afternoon, packing our boxes on a lighter, ready to take to the *Sydenham* as soon as she appears.

Thursday Sept. 13th
Not allowed out today.

The *Sydenham* sailed into the harbour this afternoon and anchored about one mile from the depot.

We had the news this afternoon that the *Sydenham* was damaged by a storm in the channel. Most of her fixtures such as sheep, pig, and fowl boxes, WC's and bathrooms were swept off her decks, her bows were also damaged, so she had to put back to London to be repaired. She was within eleven miles of Plymouth last Monday and there being no wind, she was floated out to sea by the tide.

In the evening the depot master gave us a musical entertainment; the following is an account copied from the *Plymouth News Sept. 14th* "Concert at the Plymouth Emigration Depot: Mr and Mrs Grant, superintendant and matron of the Plymouth emigration depot, last evening, arranged an excellent musical concert for the benefit of the emigrants who at present occupy the establishment. The emigrants, some hundreds in number, are about to leave for Sydney in the ship *Sydenham* but are now detained through stress of weather. For their especial amusement, Mr Grant was yesterday able to secure the voluntary services of several ladies and gentlemen in the town and a thoroughly enjoyable concert was the result.

"Mrs Able and the Misses Clements and Messrs P. B. Clemens, W. Hearder, G. Pearse, W. E. Rendal and Bennet all gave their aid and one or two of the emigrants helped to give a variety to the programme, amongst the latter John Freeman and his son, a lad of eight years, gave a duet on the cornet and Lawrence MacGowen, another emigrant, was among the vocalists. Each acquitted himself well and secured the hearty plaudits of the crowded audience. The other artists went through an

excellent performance to the delights of the emigrants whose demands for encores afforded ample evidence of their thorough appreciation of the efforts which were made to please them.

"They will all embark today under the superintendance of Mr Hughes Phillips, dispatching officer for New South Wales. They will be accompanied in the ship by Dr Pearce as medical officer, and Mrs Goodman as matron."

This being our last night on shore, we had a jolly spree in our bedroom until near morning, the constables being no good at all.

Friday Sept. 14th

All busy this morning preparing for our departure, our boxes were taken away at six a.m.

We left the depot at eleven a.m. by the *Sir Walter Raleigh*, a small steamer which conveyed us to the *Sydenham*. We dined on board, having roast beef, soup, and potatoes. As soon as dinner was over, a clergyman came on board and gave us a farewell sermon. He also spoke on temperance, bringing with him some pledge cards; many signed them, I was among the number.

The single men occupied the fore hatch, the length being fifty-eight feet, width at the fore end twenty feet six inches and thirty-two feet six inches the lower end. This was occupied by one hundred and fifteen single men (or they were booked as single men, five or six turned out to be married and had left their wives at home). The married people occupied the main hatch and the single girls abaft. The latter were not allowed off the poop from the time they went on the vessel, until they arrived at Sydney. The single men not being allowed past the married peoples' quarters only on Sunday to Church service and also when there was a concert held on the quarter deck, so that no communication could be carried on between the single women and the single men.

Three of the single men were appointed as constables over us, their duty being to see that we received our full amount of provisions and behaved ourselves, the penalty for offenders being their bread stopped for a week. The doctor appointed eight men every morning to clean the deck of our hatch, the constables had to see that it was done properly. The deck had to be swept, scraped, swept, sanded, and holy-stoned, and swept again, every morning after breakfast, four of the same men having to sweep the deck after dinner, the other four to carry water for the cook. Three more men having to watch through the night from nine till six a.m. each man watching three hours and reporting to the officer of the ship whether all is well or not in the fore hatch. The constables wore a badge on their arm, with the initials S. M. C. woven in, they received three pounds at the end of the voyage for their duties.

Three married men were appointed constables over the married people, their duties being the same as the single men constables. Three married men were also appointed as constables for the single girls, their duties being to carry provisions to the girls from the stores and galley. Three single women were appointed as sub–matrons, their duty being to keep order among the single women only. One married man was appointed as lamp-lighter, his duty was to keep the lanterns clean and to light and extinguish them at the proper time. Another married man was appointed as water closet constable. Each constable received three pounds for their duties.

We were supposed to have fire drill once a week, the single and married men were divided in gangs, about twenty in each, each gang under an officer or able seaman, our duty being in case of fire, to work the pumps and pass water to where it was needed. We had two very narrow escapes from fire, the cooks' galley caught on fire late one night, through some wood being left near the stove. It was extinguished by a few who were on deck, happily before an alarm was created. The other occasion was through a man's pipe being put in his bunk before it was extinguished.

We had fresh beef for three days after leaving Plymouth, after which we had a weekly allowance, according to the following scale:

Per week per statute adult:

Beef or pork, or partly one and partly the other: 2lbs 4ozs
Preserved meat: 1lb 0ozs
Suet: 0lbs 6ozs
Butter: 0lbs 4ozs
Bread or biscuit not inferior to navy biscuit: 2lbs 8ozs
Wheaten flour not inferior to best seconds: 3lbs 8ozs
Oatmeal, Rice, and Peas, or any two of them: 2lbs 0ozs
Potatoes: 2lbs 0ozs
Raisins: 0lbs 6ozs
Tea: 0lbs 2ozs
Sugar: 1lb 0ozs
Salt: 0lbs 2ozs
Mustard: 0lbs ½ oz
Pepper black or white: 0lbs ½oz
Preserved and dried vegetables; } Two portions
Cabbage, carrot, turnip, onion, celery, mint. }
Vinegar or mixed pickle: 1 gill

Our food was divided out in the following manner:
Sunday: Preserved beef or mutton, potatoes and onions.
Monday: Salt junk and preserved carrots.
Tuesday: Salt pork and pea soup.
Wednesday: Preserved beef or mutton and potatoes.
Thursday: Salt junk and preserved carrots.
Friday: Preserved beef or mutton and potatoes.
Saturday: Salt pork and pea soup.

We had rice and porridge alternately every morning but Mondays and Thursdays for breakfast. The fresh potatoes did not last many weeks, after which we had to resort to preserved potatoes which was very similar to boiled sawdust.

Each man was allowed 10ozs of fresh bread per day and as many navy biscuits as we could eat. We used them for cakes and puddings, we broke them into small pieces with a hammer and soaked them in water for 12hrs, then mixed them with flour. We did not eat them because we were fond of them, our motto was, "what don't fat fills." We would manage to have a small cake every day with biscuits, or if we wanted a treat on Sundays, we would save our flour through the week and have a pie with preserved beef or mutton, which was the best feed we could get.

We held a few demonstrations on the bread question, as we never got our right allowance, after which we went in a mob to the cabin and demanded more bread off the doctor, his answer was eat more biscuits. The captain told us we would eat a horse and cart, if it was on board, some conspired to kill the cat, but failing means of cooking her afterwards, that question was dropped. So we contented ourselves by going to bed and, like the men we were, only dreamed we were hungry. We had good reason to complain of the short allowance of bread, because much later on we found that the crew used our rations.

Saturday Sept. 15th

At five o'clock on the morning of the fifteenth of September Eighteen Eighty Three, we were awoke by the sailors who were busy weighing the anchor, at the same time singing the anchor shanty. We were all very soon on deck, lending them a helping hand. As soon as the anchor was up and made fast to the cathead, a hauser was passed out to a steam tug which was waiting alongside and made fast to her, she then started tugging us out to sea.

The morning was foggy so we soon lost sight of old England. Everyone seemed quite jolly, with the exception of a few females, who added a little more water to the briny deep, thinking there was not enough to sail our ship. We passed by the noble Eddystone, there are some awful dangerous rocks round it.

The steam tug left us about one mile south of the Eddystone lighthouse, then the sails were unfurled, the anchors weighed. "Farewell, farewell," was sung by some of the young men, after which, we went below with a good appetite.

There was scarcely a breeze of wind blowing all day, so we made but little progress towards getting over the sixteen thousand miles which are now before us. The day passed very pleasantly, as everything was new to us landlubbers, we sighted a vessel in the channel, after which they were few and far between. The ship was very steady, so we didn't feel sick in the least. In the evening we had a concert on the forecastle head, some of the sailors adding to the programme.

Sunday Sept. 16th

Weather fine, slight breeze.

We had the Church service read by the doctor at eleven a.m. on the quarter deck, using the single girls' hatchway with the Union Jack spread over it for a pulpit. The Roman Catholics held their service in the forehatch. It seemed very unlike the Sabbath day, having no church service and not being able to go for walks afterwards because the roads were slopey.

Monday Sept. 17th

Weather stormy, strong breeze blowing.

The S. S. Sydenham measured two hundred and twenty feet long, thirty-eight feet wide, forty feet from the keel to the main deck and one hundred and ninety feet from the main deck to the top of the main mast. The crew consisted of twenty-six able and ordinary seamen, this being a double crew to what they would have if they had no passengers. Boatswain, Carpenter, Sailmaker, Engineer, First, Second and Third Mates, Two Stewards, Two Cooks, One Baker and Alexandra Ross the Captain. The Sydenham carried six life boats, each boat having a keg of fresh water in case we were wrecked.

Our vessel pitched and rolled today for the first time, which made most of us begin casting up our accounts; it was amusing to see all of us hanging our heads over the bulwarks, shooting the cat. Many a bitter curse the sailors gave us today, they had all their work cut out to keep the decks clean. We stayed on deck till late at night.

We are on the western borders of the Bay of Biscay.

Church service could not be held today.

103

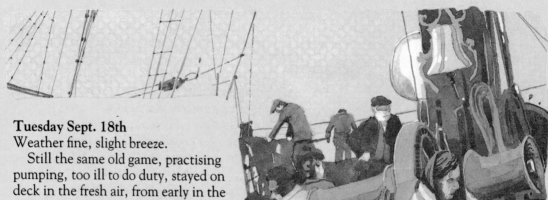

Tuesday Sept. 18th
Weather fine, slight breeze.

Still the same old game, practising pumping, too ill to do duty, stayed on deck in the fresh air, from early in the morning, until late at night. Between decks is very disagreeable, with the smell of sickness and disinfecting powder. The doctor, and the Captain, examines our hatch every morning, as soon as it is cleaned.

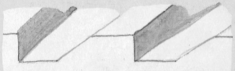

Thursday Sept. 20th
Weather very stormy.

We are now beginning to feel a most ravenous appetite, which is not to be appeased by the scanty allowance that we are allowed. Once again we complained to the doctor, but it was no use, his heart was hardened, if he had one at all. Some wished they were back with Old John and his roast beef.

Sunday Sept. 23rd
Weather very rough.

We had a very heavy storm, it lasted most of the day. Some of us wished we were back on dry land, for we thought we were all going to the fishes. The waves were continually sweeping the deck of the ship, the fore mainsail was split with the wind. Although it was amusing at meal times to see our pannikins and plates tossed in all directions when a wave gave us a broadside, we now understand why we were issued with tin-ware.

About five o'clock in the evening the wind dropped suddenly which was almost as bad as the storm, because the sea was very rough, which made the vessel roll fearfully, there being no wind to steady her.

Monday Sept. 24th
Weather fair, good breeze.
  A child died this evening.

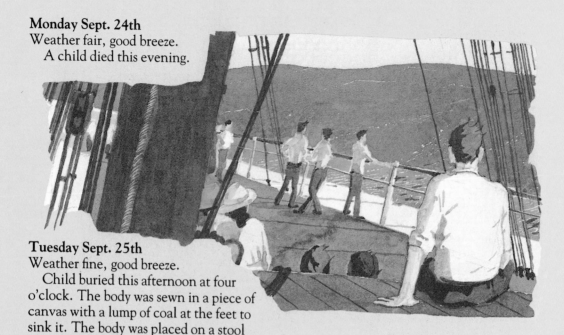

Tuesday Sept. 25th
Weather fine, good breeze.
  Child buried this afternoon at four
o'clock. The body was sewn in a piece of
canvas with a lump of coal at the feet to
sink it. The body was placed on a stool
covered with a Union Jack, the doctor
read the burial service and as the service
was finished, the body was dropped in
the water.

Wednesday Sept. 26th
Weather fine. Fair wind.
  Our amusement throughout the day is
generally reading or writing, writing
being very difficult when the vessel is
rolling. Our evening sports are mostly
leap frog, hide and seek, touch,
draughts, tip it and catching the wrong
pigs by the ear. On moonlight nights
there was mostly music and dancing on
deck.
  Our lights were all extinguished by
ten p.m. excepting one for the
watchmen. After the lights were
extinguished we used to pelt each other
with the hard ship's biscuits, always
taking a good supply of ammunition to
our bunks. Sometimes the constables
would get out in their night shirts to try
and stop it which of course would cause
more amusement, they being good
targets for our sport.

Tuesday Oct. 2nd
Weather showery.
  Passed two vessels, distance 208 miles.
  We are now having some very hot
weather, we complained to the doctor
for not having enough ventilation in the
fore hatch. We asked him to have the
Issuing room taken out of our hatch.
This was a room about 7ft square placed
at the end of our hatch to hold
provisions and it stopped the fresh air
from circulating through our bunks. The
doctor would not have it down so me
and six others started pulling the place
down. We were stopped by the Mate,
our names were taken and threatened
with imprisonment when we arrived at
Sydney.
  It all turned out to be very handy
afterwards, as we could always have milk
in our teas and a rice pudding
occasionally. It's an ill wind that blows
no one good. After we complained we
had some wind sails put up, to carry the
wind down the hatch which made
things so much better. Some of the men
slept on deck when it was fine.

Wednesday Oct. 3rd

Weather stormy.

Distance 244 miles.

We saw some flying fish, they are about the size of a mackerel, they fly a long distance over the water, a few fell on deck and were specially devoured by the natives. The doctor told us to get our letters ready to send home, as they expected to pass a steamer homeward bound, so we were all very busy writing letters but we never had a chance to send them.

A child died today.

Saturday Oct. 13th

Weather fine, hot, and calm.

Saw a large shark this morning, followed by four or five pilot fish which are about the size of mackerel.

Slight breeze this evening.

Latitude 8% North

Distance travelled since last Sunday noon, is 189 miles.

Monday Oct. 22nd

Weather fine, good breeze.

We crossed the equator today, the sailors had a spree in the evening, they let off a few fireworks and were answered by a ship on the starboard beams. After the fireworks, Father Neptune made his appearance on deck and pity the man who was on deck after that. A few were caught and received a good ducking.

When we were all below, the sailors threw water down the hatch until they were exhausted.

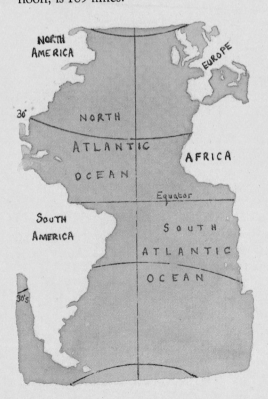

107

Wednesday Nov. 21st
Weather wet, fair wind.
  Distance 172 miles.
  Latitude 42° 25 m Longitude 22° 2m
  Course South 7 pts East
  Fire brigade called out to drill at 4 p.m.
  We had a very heavy storm in the night. The main top gallant, the fore top gallant and one stay sail was carried away. We were obliged to stay below for fear of being washed overboard, tons of water were sweeping her decks from stem to stern, every moment we thought we were going under. It was a fearful rough night, the vessel shook and trembled as though she would break in pieces.
  A child was born in the night.
  We were running before a gale of wind all night long.

Thursday Dec. 6th
Weather rough, head wind.
  Distance 55 miles.
  The wind was blowing a hurricane all day. We made but little progress as it was a head wind.
  Another terrific storm in the night, the fore top stay sail was carried away, it sounded like the report of a cannon. The sailors could not find out which one it was till morning as it was so dark, when they found a few rags of sail left.
  A child died in the night.

Tuesday Dec. 11th
Weather fine, calm.
  Carpenter busy making new yard.
  A school of whales round our vessel spouting, it looked like a lot of fountains playing. A large one came close to the bows of our vessel, he came to the top, spouted, then gave a grunt and disappeared. He smelled very oily and measured between thirty and forty feet.
  Six albatross caught today, the largest measured 11ft 6 ins across the wings.
  Child buried this afternoon.

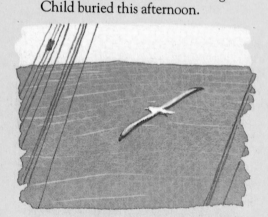

Friday Dec. 21st
All excited, expecting to see Sydney in a few days.
  All busy scrubbing and cleaning our hatch, so as to be respectable when we enter Port Jackson.

Monday Dec. 24th
Weather fine, good breeze.
  The doctor allowed us to have our boxes up today.
  Extra fruit and flour served out today for our Christmas pudding.
  Concert in the fore hatch, Christmas Eve.

Tuesday Dec. 25th

Christmas Day.

"Land ahead" was shouted by the man on the look out at break of day. It passed through the vessel like an electric shock and in a few minutes were were all straining our eyes to see the long promised land. The officers were all busy taking soundings, they had to stop the ship because she was running straight for land. We saw the light from Sydney lighthouse as it revolved, we were then about seventy miles from Sydney.

We sailed along in sight of land till eleven a.m. when we were opposite the Heads, which are two high rocks, one on each side of the harbour mouth. The Captain then signalled for a tug which we soon saw coming towards us, also another steamer which was bringing a pilot who was soon on our vessel. A cord was thrown to the tug boat with a hauser attached to it which was soon made fast to the tug and then we soon found ourselves in Sydney Harbour.

We dropped anchor in the quarantine quarters for inspection. After dinner a doctor came on board to examine us. He found us all well and healthy, with the exception of two children who had the whooping cough, for which we had to stay in quarantine for four days.

It was a lovely day and we had a splendid view around us, in fact we were completely shut in from the Pacific. The harbour was full of mackerel it being the season for them here, so we amused ourselves fishing.

We had a very happy Christmas, finishing with a concert on the quarter deck. The harbour was full of pleasure boats decked with flags and flowers.

Wednesday Dec. 26th

Weather fine and warm.

Our boxes brought up and examined by the Custom House officers.

All busy washing today, all sheets and linen had to be soaked in carbolic acid for two hours. They made us washermen.

Thursday Dec. 27th

Weather showery.

All busy washing, a bad day for drying; we don't trouble which way the wind blows.

Friday Dec. 28th

Weather fine.

All the hatches fumigated today with brimstone, no treacle used. After it was over, we were towed into Neutral Bay and anchored there. In the evening we had a lecture delivered to us on New South Wales, advising us to go up the country.

We were allowed to stay seven clear days on the *Sydenham* after anchoring in Neutral Bay.

Concert aft in the evening.

Saturday Dec. 29th

Weather fine.

The single girls were taken to the Government depot this morning at 8 o'clock. Government Officers came on board and asked us all if we were satisfied with our treatment on the voyage, no complaints were made.

At two p.m. a small steamer came and took all who liked to go on shore free! Most of us were glad of the chance to get on land after one hundred and six days on the water.

As soon as we landed at the circular quay, we made our way to the G. P. O. for letters, after which we walked through the town until 9 p.m. when we went back to the *Sydenham* in high glee and many drunk (no doubt they were glad to get some drink after so long a drought).

Sunday Dec. 30th

Weather fine, very hot.

Morning service held on the quarter deck, conducted by the secretary of the Y.M.C.A.

In the middle of the night, the *Sydenham* began to drag her anchor, having only her port anchor down. The sailors were all called out to cast the starboard anchor and after a deal of trouble, they succeeded in getting the anchor cast, but not before we were within twenty yards of the rocks.

Monday Dec. 31st

Weather fine.

At 9 a.m. a steamer took us to the hiring room, which is for farmers to hire labourers. The N.S.W. Government gave each man six shillings for his bed because they were to be destroyed on account of having to lay in quarantine. Free passes were given to anyone who wanted to go up the country. Twelve got passes for Goulburn, myself among the number, to start from Sydney at 8.30. p.m.

We went back to the *Sydenham* and got our luggage ready, and about 3 p.m. we had the pleasure of wishing the *Sydenham* farewell.

Eight children died during that long voyage and two others were born. And my uncle Will? Well, he stayed in Australia for a few years doing various things such as prospecting for gold for a short while. He came back to England to be married and he died in 1934, aged seventy-one.

HOME-GROWN WORDS

Glossary

bindis *(p.27)*
small Australian bushes bearing fruit with prickly husks or burrs

bluff *(p.52)*
steep headland

bulwarks *(p.103)*
part of a ship's side, above the upper deck

cathead *(p.103)*
a beam projecting outwards from the bow of a ship as a support to lift the anchor

chaffered *(p.83)*
bargained

chaise *(p.46)*
open carriage

conniving *(p.86)*
scheming

convalescent *(p.55)*
recovering health after being ill

convenience *(p.97)*
toilet

flitch *(p.80)*
side

hauser *(p.103)*
hawser; a cable or rope

holystoned *(p.101)*
cleaning the wooden decks with a piece of soft sandstone

lighter *(p.99)*
a large barge used to transport goods over short distances

Glossary continues on page 112

pannikins *(p.104)*
small saucepans or metal cups

poop *(p.101)*
the deck at the stern of a ship above the main deck

roan cob *(p.46)*
short-legged stocky horse with white or grey markings

temperance *(p.101)*
giving up alcoholic drinks

tracts *(p.98)*
papers or pamphlets

ute *(p.28)*
short for utility. In Australia a car that has room for driver and one passenger with room to carry things in the back.

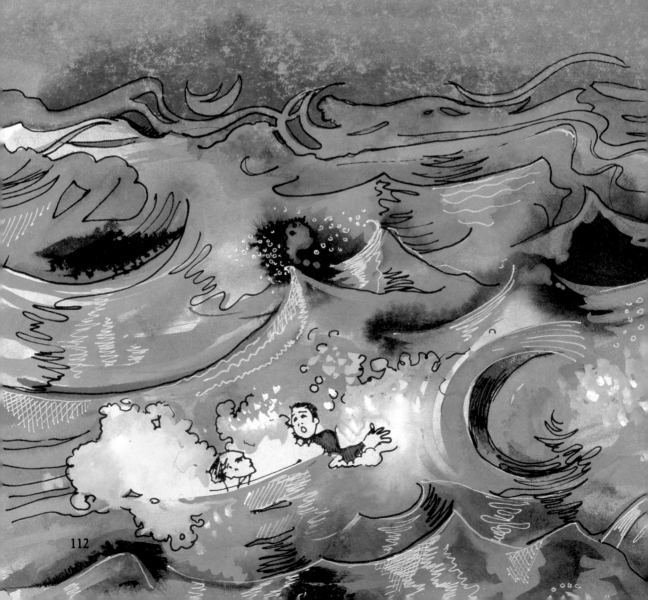